FROM FREEZER, 'FRIDGE AND PANTRY

Eugenia Branscomb Hobday

BRISTOL PUBLISHING ENTERPRISES
San Leandro, California

a nitty gritty® cookbook

Printed in the United States of America.

ISBN 1-55867-169-2

Cover design: Frank J. Paredes
Cover photography: John A. Benson
Food stylist: Susan Massey
Illustrator: James Balkovek

CONTENTS

To everyone who has made my task easier, I offer a special thank you.

I am particularly indebted to home economists Mary Ellen Jenks and Bonnie Peterson formerly of the Green Giant Company; Florence Rasch and Sally Henderson from the University of North Alabama; Harriet Babin Miller, Charlotte Gandy, Charlotte Pheifer, Melba Price, Ludwika Yoes and Dee Wellan.

I would also like to thank Margene Beckham, Marie Branscomb, Mary Bryant, Bonnie and Jan Howle, Babe Martin and Regina Schaub.

Thanks to the Mirro Corporation for providing bakeware to use in testing.

Thanks to typists Natalie Branscomb, Penny Leggett and Tiffany Howle.

My heartfelt appreciation goes to my family, especially my father and my sister, and the Brent Yoes family, whose love, ongoing encouragement and practical assistance made this book possible.

CAN-DO COOKING

Does a busy schedule or a change of plans throw you into a tizzy at mealtime? Do unexpected guests send you dashing to the nearest fast-food restaurant or delicatessen? Relax! With a supply of prepared frozen, refrigerated and canned foods on hand, panic will change to pleasure as tasty dishes seem to leap from the shelf. Many of these recipes directly combine a can, bottle or jar of this and a carton and package of that. Others require some additional preparation, but it can often be done ahead of time. The use of convenience foods reduces the number of ingredients needed and much of the time-consuming shopping and preparation. Most of the ingredients can be kept on hand for long periods of time, ready to whip together in a few minutes.

For many recipes, only a single container is needed. As a result, they are ideal for use by busy families, singles, twosomes, seniors, campers and yachtsmen — those who want a good meal quickly with a minimum of preparation and cleanup. This approach also appeals to those who lack the time, inclination or skills to prepare a variety of dishes from scratch. These dishes are easily doubled or tripled for family gatherings or entertaining. Many of the simple-to-follow recipes are suitable for children to make.

This cookbook's "out of the can and into the pan" methods will be your primary resource of easy-to-assemble, short-order recipes for every course.

THE PANIC BUTTON PANTRY

The fast pace of today's lifestyle means there's less time and energy for food shopping, preparation and cooking. Convenience foods can save precious minutes by cutting down on ingredients and preparation tasks. "Fresh is best" is a great philosophy, but today's cooks encounter occasions when the ease and speed of "panic button" cooking is invaluable. With the profusion of instant, canned, frozen, dried, powdered and concentrated food now available, the ingredients for a variety of dishes can be kept within arm's reach in the kitchen.

To ensure healthful eating and to arrive at the best cost per serving, become a zealous label reader. Compare brands and check the unit price cost in front of the shelf beneath the item. Experiment with different brands of convenience foods to determine the ones with the best flavor and quality. It's not worth buying cheaper items to save money if your recipe results suffer accordingly. Once you settle on a brand you like, check the prices periodically. If the cost plunges, it's time to stock up. If you can't locate a product, ask the store manager to order it.

Throughout this book, the can or package called for is designated by the number of ounces it contains. However, don't take this so literally that you will bypass a 15-ounce can if the 16-ounce can is not available.

TIME- AND TEMPER-SAVING TIPS

The recipes in this book have been streamlined wherever possible to help you save time and effort. Cooks on the run can speed up food preparation and cleanup time even more by referring to the following hints.

- Print a few of your favorite "panic button" recipes on index cards and attach them to the shelf above the required ingredients.
- Keep a list of the ingredients in a small notebook so you can stop by the grocery store at short notice.
- When you bring new items home from the grocery store, place frozen foods promptly in the freezer. Store canned, packaged and bottled goods in a cool, dry place. Turn labels toward the front of your shelves so you can identify them at a glance.
- Before starting a recipe, read it through completely and assemble all ingredients and equipment needed.
- Begin meal preparation with the food that takes the longest to cook. Turn the oven or broiler on to preheat, or start heating the water to cook rice or noodles before opening cans or combining ingredients.

- Invest in an audible kitchen timer, if you don't have one on your stove, to remind you when a dish should be checked or removed from the refrigerator, stovetop or oven.

- Need cooked chicken for a recipe? Place 4 skinned and boned chicken breast halves in a shallow microwavable glass baking dish. Cover with waxed paper. Microwave on HIGH for 5 to 7 minutes per pound, turning over halfway through cooking time. Or, bake at 325° for 20 minutes or until done. Cool and cube.

- Several different sources exist for purchasing cooked chicken. Grocery stores offer refrigerated ready-cooked chicken pieces and Cornish game hens. Fried chicken is available in the frozen food section. Whole ready-cooked chicken can be purchased from a supermarket 's service deli or an independent delicatessen. Ready-to-eat fried chicken is available from fast food restaurants.

- To make zero-fat popcorn with zero cleanup, place about ¼ cup popping corn in a paper lunch bag. Seal it tightly by folding over the edges several times and creasing them well. Lay the bag on its side in the microwave oven. Microwave on HIGH for 3 to 4 minutes or until the popping subsides. Be careful as you open the bag to avoid getting burned by escaping steam.

- The quickest dessert is a purchased one. Many desserts can also be served as afternoon snacks or party treats. Some can be prepared ahead of time and tucked away in the freezer for quick use.

- You can often avoid washing an extra dish by mixing the ingredients directly in the casserole, pot or other cooking container.

- For easier cleanup, lightly spray casseroles or baking dishes with nonstick cooking spray before adding the ingredients. Or, use aluminum foil as a disposable liner.

- To easily clean your blender or food processor, partially fill the container with hot water and add a drop of detergent. Cover and turn on the appliance for about ten seconds. Rinse and air dry.

- Cold drinks and salads taste twice as refreshing if the glasses, plates or bowls are chilled before using.

- Use an electric heating tray to warm dinner plates and serving dishes, or to keep prepared items at the proper serving temperature.

TIPS FOR FROZEN FOODS

- Frozen packages should be firm and clean, without an ice coating or discoloration from the contents, which indicates previous thawing and refreezing.

- Today's frozen fish and shellfish are high in nutritional value, low in calories and economical because there is little waste. Most are quick-frozen within a very short time of being caught, so their fresh flavor and nutrients are retained.

- To thaw frozen broccoli, green beans or spinach, place them in the refrigerator overnight on a plate. Or, microwave on HIGH for 2 minutes or until soft, turning package over after 1 minute. Drain in a colander. Press spinach with the back of a large spoon to extract as much moisture as possible.

- To separate frozen vegetables quickly, pour boiling water over them in a colander. To thaw frozen vegetables to use raw, run cold water over them in a colander for a few minutes.

- When barbecuing, place the unthawed contents of a 10-ounce package of frozen vegetables on a large square of heavy-duty aluminum foil. Season with salt and pepper and top with a pat or two of butter or margarine. Bring the edges of foil up and, leaving a little space for expansion of steam, seal tightly with a double fold in the center and at the ends. Place package on the grill over white-hot coals and cook for about 25 minutes, turning occasionally. To double the amount, prepare two separate packages of vegetables instead of one large package.

TIPS FOR REFRIGERATED FOODS

- Fresh parsley, mint, chives or other herbs provide a colorful garnish for convenience food dishes. To prepare, snip the desired amount directly over the dish with kitchen shears.

- To save preparation work, take advantage of the trimmed and ready-cut fruits and vegetables available in produce sections and supermarket salad bars. The vegetables can be used for a quick stir-fry or veggie-topped pizza.

- Washed, ready-to-use packaged fresh spinach and salad mixtures can go directly into a salad bowl and onto the dinner table.

- A wide selection of cheese is available sliced, shredded, in blocks, in links and in various containers. Cheese can be served with crackers or fruit for an instant appetizer, snack or dessert. It can also be used to enhance a variety of dishes, as it contributes flavor, color and nutrients.

TIPS FOR CANNED FOODS

- Avoid canned goods that are dented, leaking, swollen or bulging at either end.

- Before opening a can of condensed soup, shake it well.

- Reserve the juice from canned fruits to replace all or some of the water called for in recipes for beverages, gelatin salads, brownies, cakes or muffins.

- Use the liquid drained from canned vegetables to add extra flavor and nutrition to homemade soups, gravies and sauces.

- Save the liquid from canned tomatoes and the water in which vegetables are cooked and add to soups for additional flavor and nutrients.

- Kitchen shears make quick work of chopping canned tomatoes. Insert shears into the open can, snipping the tomatoes into smaller pieces.

- Sweetened condensed milk and evaporated milk are entirely different products and cannot be used interchangeably.

- Use a fork when removing chicken, ham, tuna or turkey from a can to break it up into bite-sized pieces.

- Canned seafood is among the most popular of all convenience foods. Reach for a can when guests arrive unexpectedly or when you are short of time. For fresher flavor, rinse seafood with cold water in a sieve; drain well.

- Canned foods can be heated in their containers, which is especially convenient when camping or for a cookout. Remove the lid to prevent pressure buildup and cover can loosely with aluminum foil. Place can in a saucepan of hot water and simmer until heated through. Or, remove the labels from cans, open cans almost all the way, leaving the lid in place for a cover. Place the can on the grill over hot coals. When heated through, drain and add flavorings such as butter or seasonings. You may need to add a little water or other liquid.
- Never place an unopened can on a heat source or put the can in the microwave.
- Remember to use hot pads or large tongs to handle hot cans.

BEVERAGES

ICERS

To avoid diluting cold drinks, use one of the following instead of ice cubes. Add to beverages containing compatible ingredients just before serving.

FRUIT JUICE CUBES: Fill ice cube trays or miniature muffin cups with cranberry juice cocktail, fruit juice or fruit nectar. Freeze until solid. Pineapple juice cubes are especially good in iced tea.

FROZEN FRUIT SPARKLERS: Pour lemon-lime soda or ginger ale into ice cube trays or miniature muffin cups. Place a drained maraschino cherry, Mandarin orange segment or pineapple chunk into each section. Freeze until solid.

FRUIT-FLAVORED CUBES: Reconstitute frozen juice concentrates according to the directions on the can. Pour into ice cube trays or miniature muffin cups. Freeze until solid.

FROZEN FRUIT: Arrange drained, canned Mandarin orange segments, pineapple chunks and/or maraschino cherries in a single layer on a foil-covered baking sheet. Or, use bunches of green or purple grapes, or red apple slices. Freeze until solid. Store in locking freezer bags.

CAN-OPENER COCKTAIL

Serve this tasty concoction as an informal first course. This recipe is also delicious served hot: simmer ingredients in a 1-quart saucepan, stirring occasionally, until heated through. Serve hot cocktail in 3 small mugs or bouillon cups.

1 can (11.5 oz.) vegetable juice, such as V-8
1 can (10.75 oz.) condensed beef broth
lemon wedges for garnish, optional

Pour ingredients into a 1-quart jar or container with a tight-fitting lid. Cover securely and shake vigorously until well blended. Refrigerate until well chilled. Shake mixture before serving. Serve in 6-ounce glasses over ice, garnished with lemon wedges if desired.

VARIATION: SPICY TOMATO-CLAM COCKTAIL

Substitute spicy-hot vegetable juice or bloody Mary cocktail mix for vegetable juice; substitute 1 bottle (8 oz.) clam juice for beef broth.

CREAMY ORANGE SHAKE

This creamy, sweet treat doubles as both a beverage and a dessert. If desired, you can substitute 1 can (14 oz.) sweetened condensed milk for the vanilla pie filling and whipped topping mix.

1 can (6 oz.) frozen orange juice concentrate
1 cup cold water
1 pkg. (3.4 oz.) instant vanilla pudding and pie filling mix
1 pkg. (1.3 oz.) whipped dessert topping mix
3 cups ice cubes

In a blender container, combine juice concentrate, cold water and vanilla pudding mix; cover and blend until smooth. Add dessert topping mix, cover and blend for 15 seconds. With the motor running on high speed, remove lid insert or lid and add about 4 ice cubes at a time. Blend after each addition until mixture is smooth and frothy. Scrape down sides of blender as necessary. Serve immediately in 8-ounce glasses.

PEACHY VANILLA SHAKE

Serve this delectable, nutritious shake as a snack or a meal on the run.

1 can (16 oz.) sliced peaches in juice
2 cups (16 oz. carton) vanilla yogurt
2 cups ice cubes

Place peaches and yogurt in a blender container; cover and blend until smooth. With the motor running on high speed, remove lid insert or lid and add about 4 ice cubes at a time. Blend after each addition until mixture is smooth and frothy. Serve immediately in 8-ounce glasses.

FRUIT FIZZ

Here's a refreshing, nonalcoholic bubbly drink. It's a tasty alternative to soft drinks.

1 can (12 oz.) frozen orange or other juice concentrate
1 bottle (1 liter) ginger ale, club soda or sparkling mineral water, chilled

Combine ingredients in a large pitcher, stirring gently until mixed. Serve immediately in 6-ounce glasses over crushed ice.

GOLDEN APPLE FIZZ

Double or triple the ingredients to serve as a punch.

1 can (12 oz.) frozen orange juice concentrate
1 bottle (32 oz.) apple juice, chilled
1 bottle (1 liter) ginger ale, chilled

Combine orange juice concentrate and apple juice in a large pitcher. Slowly pour ginger ale down one side of pitcher, stirring gently until mixed. Serve immediately in 6-ounce glasses over crushed ice.

LUAU LEMONADE

Here's a new approach to a family favorite. Serve the punch variation in stemmed glasses with brunch.

1 can (6 oz.) frozen lemonade concentrate
¾ cup (1 lemonade can) cold water
1 can (11.5 oz.) apricot nectar, chilled
1 can (12 oz.) unsweetened pineapple juice, chilled
1 can (12 oz.) lemon-lime soda, chilled

Combine lemonade concentrate and cold water in a large pitcher and stir until dissolved. Stir in fruit juices and lemon-lime soda. Serve immediately in 12-ounce glasses over ice.

VARIATION: LUAU FRUIT PUNCH

Servings: 15-17

Substitute 1 can (6 oz.) frozen orange juice concentrate for lemonade concentrate, and 1 bottle (750 ml.) dry white sparkling wine or champagne, chilled, for lemon-lime soda. Serve in 6-ounce glasses over ice.

CRANBERRY SPRITZER

This nonalcoholic cocktail has a delightful tang. Serve it to designated drivers at a cocktail party.

1 can (6 oz.) frozen limeade or lemonade concentrate
1 bottle (32 oz.) cranberry juice cocktail, chilled
1 bottle (1 liter) ginger ale, chilled

Combine limeade concentrate with cranberry juice in a large pitcher and stir to mix well. Slowly pour ginger ale down one side of pitcher and stir gently to mix. Serve immediately in 12-ounce glasses over ice.

MULLED GRAPE NECTAR

Servings: 12-15

Serve this delicious beverage by the fire on a cold day.

1 can (46 oz.) white grape juice
1 can (46 oz.) apricot or pear nectar

1 jar (about 1 oz.) whole stick cinnamon

In a 5-quart saucepan or Dutch oven, combine grape juice and nectar. Bring mixture to a boil, stirring occasionally. Pour into a heatproof pitcher, punch bowl or soup tureen. Serve warm in 8-ounce mugs with cinnamon stick stirrers.

COLD WEATHER CIDER

Servings: 22-24

The cinnamon flavor comes from melted red hot candies.

1 bottle (64 oz.) apple cider or juice
1 can (12 oz.) frozen orange juice
concentrate

2½ cups water
¼ cup red hot cinnamon candy pieces

In a 5-quart saucepan or Dutch oven, combine apple cider, orange juice concentrate and water. Add candy pieces and bring to a boil. Reduce heat to low and simmer for 10 minutes, stirring occasionally, until candy is melted. Pour into a heatproof pitcher, punch bowl or soup tureen. Serve warm in 6-ounce mugs.

HOT CHOCOLATE MIX

Keep this popular treat on hand for camping, cookouts or to give as gifts. As needed, place 3 to 4 tbs. chocolate mix in a mug. Add 1 cup boiling water and stir until dissolved. For a special treat, garnish mugs of hot chocolate with a peppermint stick, marshmallows or whipped cream.

1 box (16 oz.) confectioners' sugar
1 box (25.6 oz.) nonfat dry milk
1 box (14.5-15 oz.) instant chocolate-flavored drink powder
1 jar (6 oz.) nondairy creamer

If necessary, sift confectioners' sugar to remove lumps. Combine all ingredients in a large bowl, mixing well. Store in a tightly covered container in a cool, dry place.

GOLDEN GLOW PUNCH

This hot-weather treat can easily be adjusted to serve to large groups. It can also be mixed in a 4-quart pitcher and served as a refreshing drink in ice-filled glasses.

1 can (11.5 oz.) apricot nectar, chilled
1 can (46 oz.) unsweetened pineapple juice, chilled
1 bottle (1 liter) ginger ale, chilled
choice of *Icers:* 1-2 trays *Fruit Juice Cubes, Frozen Fruit Sparklers* or *Fruit-Flavored Cubes,* or 2 cups *Frozen Fruit,* page 11

Combine juices in a large punch bowl. Slowly pour ginger ale down one side of bowl, stirring gently until mixed. Add *Icers* and serve immediately in 4-ounce cups.

VARIATION: CITRUS PUNCH
Servings: 28-30

Substitute the following for apricot nectar: 1 can (12 oz.) frozen orange juice concentrate, 1 can (12 oz.) frozen lemonade concentrate and $1\frac{1}{2}$ cups (1 juice can) cold water.

CRANBERRY-APPLE PUNCH

The tangy flavor of this sparkling drink will please any group.

1 can (6 oz.) frozen lemonade concentrate
1 bottle (64 oz.) cranberry apple or cranberry juice cocktail, chilled
1 bottle (1 liter) club soda, chilled
choice of *Icers:* 1-2 trays *Fruit Juice Cubes, Frozen Fruit Sparklers* or *Fruit-Flavored Cubes*, or 2 cups *Frozen Fruit*, page 11

Combine lemonade concentrate with juice cocktail in a large punch bowl, stirring until well mixed. Slowly pour club soda down one side of bowl, stirring gently until mixed. Add *Icer*s and serve immediately in 4-ounce cups.

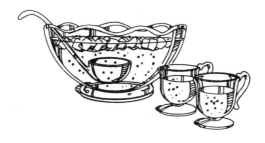

STRAWBERRY FIZZ PUNCH

Servings: 23-25

This refreshing concoction is delicious served as a party beverage or appetizer soup.

3 pkg. (10 oz. each) frozen sliced strawberries, partially thawed

1 bottle (48 oz.) white grape juice, chilled
1 bottle (1 liter) club soda, chilled

Place 2 pkg. of the strawberries, including syrup, in a blender container. Cover and blend until smooth. Combine blended strawberries, grape juice and remaining strawberries in a large punch bowl. Slowly pour club soda down one side of bowl, stirring gently with an up-and-down motion until mixed. Serve immediately in 4-ounce cups.

TROPICAL TREAT PUNCH

Servings: 20-22

This punch adds a Caribbean touch to a weekend brunch or patio party.

1 can (46 oz.) unsweetened pineapple juice, chilled
1 can (15 oz.) cream of coconut, well shaken

1 can (12 oz.) frozen orange juice concentrate, thawed
7½ cups (5 juice cans) ice water

Combine pineapple juice and cream of coconut in a large punch bowl. Just before serving, add orange juice concentrate and ice water, stirring until well mixed. Serve immediately in 4-ounce cups.

ORANGE BLOSSOM PUNCH

This inexpensive punch adds a touch of elegance to a brunch, wedding or any other joyous event. The concentrates and ice water can be combined ahead of time in a large pitcher and refrigerated until serving time.

1 can (12 oz.) frozen orange juice concentrate
1 can (6 oz.) frozen lemonade concentrate
6 cups ice water
1 bottle (750 ml.) dry white sparkling wine or champagne, chilled
2 cups *Frozen Fruit*, page 11

Combine concentrates and water in a large punch bowl, stirring until well mixed. Slowly pour sparkling wine down one side of bowl, stirring gently until mixed. Add *Frozen Fruit* and serve immediately in 4-ounce cups.

APPETIZERS, SNACKS AND LIGHT MEALS

MARINATED MUSHROOMS AND OLIVES

Makes about 2 cups

Serve these as a party snack or as part of an antipasto platter. Make sure you provide a container of cocktail picks for serving.

1 jar (4.5 oz.) whole mushrooms, well drained
1 jar (about 7 oz.) stuffed green olives or pitted black olives, well drained
1/2 cup Italian salad dressing

Place mushrooms and olives in a large jar or container with a tight-fitting lid. Add salad dressing. Secure lid and gently shake ingredients together until mushrooms and olives are well coated. Or, place ingredients in a large, heavy-duty locking plastic bag and toss gently until coated. Refrigerate for 2 to 3 hours or overnight, stirring occasionally.

To serve, drain mushrooms and olives and place in a small serving bowl; discard marinade.

ITALIAN CLAM DIP

Makes about 2 cups

This easy dip goes well with chips, crackers or fresh vegetables.

2 cups (16 oz. carton) sour cream
1 pkg. (0.7 oz.) dry Italian salad dressing mix
1 can (6.5 oz.) minced clams, well drained

Combine sour cream with salad dressing mix in a small bowl and blend with a fork. Add clams and stir until well mixed. Cover and chill for at least 1 hour to blend flavors.

VARIATIONS

Substitute one of the following for Italian salad dressing mix:
- 1 pkg. (1 oz.) dry ranch-style party dip mix
- 1 pkg. (1.5 oz.) dry spaghetti sauce mix
- 1 pkg. (1.4 oz.) dry vegetable soup mix

ROSY BACON-ONION DIP

This taste-tempting dip will add color to your party spread. Drain tomatoes in a strainer, pressing down with a fork to remove most of the juice. Save the tomato juice to add to homemade soup.

2 cups (16 oz. carton) sour cream
1 pkg. (1.1 oz.) dry bacon and onion ranch party dip mix
1 can (14.5 oz.) stewed tomatoes, well drained
large corn or tortilla chips

In a medium bowl, combine sour cream with dip mix and blend well. Add tomatoes and stir with a fork until well mixed. Cover and chill in the refrigerator for at least 1 hour to blend flavors. Serve with large corn or tortilla chips.

SAVORY SPINACH DIP

Makes about 3 cups

*Just before serving, spoon this dip into a hollowed-out round loaf of bread. Use the removed bread to make bread cubes for dipping. If desired, you can substitute 1 cup mayonnaise and 1 cup plain yogurt for the sour cream. Or, you can use 1 pkg. (1 oz.) dry ranch-style party dip mix instead of vegetable soup mix. To thaw spinach quickly, refer to **Tips for Frozen Foods**, page 6.*

2 cups (16 oz. carton) sour cream
1 pkg. (0.9-1.4 oz.) dry vegetable soup mix
1 pkg. (10 oz.) frozen chopped spinach, thawed
1 can (8 oz.) sliced water chestnuts, drained, chopped, optional

In a medium bowl, blend sour cream with soup mix. Drain spinach in a colander, pressing out as much liquid as possible, or squeeze dry. Add spinach and water chestnuts, if using, to sour cream mixture and stir with fork until well blended. Cover dip and chill in the refrigerator for at least 2 hours to blend flavors. Stir before serving.

LAYERED MEXICAN APPETIZER

This multicolored dip looks like it's difficult to make, yet it takes only minutes to prepare. It's perfect to serve to a crowd. Some brands of avocado dip are labeled as guacamole. Either type will work.

1 can (16 oz.) refried beans with green chiles
1 cup (8 oz. carton) refrigerated avocado dip
1 cup (8 oz. carton) sour cream
1 cup (4 oz.) shredded sharp cheddar cheese
1 jar (8 oz.) chunky salsa
1 can (4.5 oz.) chopped black olives, drained
shredded lettuce, optional
large tortilla chips

Spread refried beans on a 12-inch round serving platter or pizza plate, leaving a 1-inch border. Spread avocado dip evenly over beans. Carefully spread sour cream over avocado dip. Repeat layers with cheese, salsa and olives. If desired, fill in border with shredded lettuce. Serve with large tortilla chips.

CHILI CHEESE DIP

Makes about 2½ cups

This is standard fare for ball games and informal parties. Serve this dip surrounded by large corn or tortilla chips or crisp vegetable pieces for dipping. For an informal lunch or supper dish, serve this over baked potatoes, cornbread, rice or toast with a salad.

1 can (15 oz.) chili with beans, regular or hot
1 can (10.75 oz.) condensed cheddar cheese or nacho cheese soup

Remove any grease from the top of chili. Combine chili and soup in an electric fondue pot or heavy 1-quart saucepan. Cook over medium heat, stirring often, until heated through. Keep warm in a fondue pot, small casserole or chafing dish over low heat.

FIESTA DIP

This hearty dip is popular with teenagers. It's terrific for a football party.

1 can (30 oz.) refried beans
1 pkg. (1.25-1.5 oz.) dry taco seasoning mix
2 cups (16 oz. carton) sour cream
2 cups (8 oz.) shredded sharp cheddar cheese
large corn or tortilla chips

Heat oven to 350°. In a medium bowl, combine refried beans with taco seasoning mix. Spoon mixture into a greased 9-x-13-inch baking dish. Spread sour cream over bean mixture and sprinkle evenly with cheese. Bake uncovered for 30 minutes. Serve hot with large corn or tortilla chips.

ARTICHOKE PARMESAN DIP

Makes about 2 cups

Don't tell your guests the name of this unusual, popular dip when you serve it. They will have fun guessing the basic ingredients. Serve with snack crackers or melba rounds. The ingredients can be mixed ahead of time and baked later, but do not freeze them.

1 can (13.75-14 oz.) quartered artichoke hearts
¾ cup mayonnaise
¾ cup (3 oz.) grated Parmesan cheese
garlic powder or garlic salt to taste

Heat oven to 350°. Drain artichoke hearts in a colander, pressing leaves to remove excess liquid. Chop finely. In a 1-quart shallow casserole, combine mayonnaise and Parmesan cheese. Stir in chopped artichokes and garlic powder or salt; mix well. Bake uncovered for 20 to 30 minutes, until mixture bubbles and starts to brown on top.

PIZZA DIP

Here's something different for pizza lovers.

1 cup (8 oz. carton) sour cream
¾ cup ricotta cheese (about ½ a 15 oz. carton)
1 pkg. (2.5 oz.) dry tomato with basil soup mix
1 jar (4.5 oz.) sliced mushrooms, drained
1 cup (4 oz.) shredded mozzarella cheese
1 loaf (about 1 lb.) Italian bread, sliced

Heat oven to 350°. In a 1-quart shallow casserole, combine sour cream, ricotta cheese and soup mix. Stir in mushrooms and ¾ cup of the mozzarella cheese. Sprinkle remaining cheese over mixture. Bake uncovered for 30 minutes, until heated through. Serve with sliced Italian bread.

SNACK CRACKER CANAPES

Makes 30-34

These are popular as an appetizer or a snack. To easily shred dried beef slices, roll slices jelly roll-style and cut crosswise into narrow strips with kitchen shears.

1 jar (2.5 oz.) thinly sliced dried beef, shredded
1 cup (4 oz.) shredded cheddar cheese
1 can (2.25 oz.) sliced black olives, drained
¾ cup mayonnaise
1 pkg. (8 oz.) whole grain rye crisp crackers or whole wheat wafers

Heat oven to 375°. In a small bowl, combine shredded beef, cheese, olives and mayonnaise until well blended. Spread a layer of beef mixture on each cracker and place on a large ungreased baking sheet. Bake for 5 to 7 minutes or until topping is hot and bubbly. Serve warm.

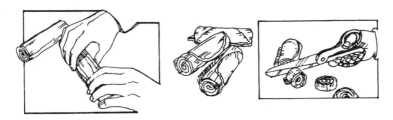

SMOKED OYSTER BITES

This recipe is easy to double and can be assembled several hours ahead of time. Cover and refrigerate until ready to bake. Large oysters should be cut in half before using.

1 can (3.75 oz.) medium-sized smoked oysters (20 oysters)
1 can (5 biscuits) refrigerated flaky buttermilk biscuits

Heat oven to 450°. Drain oysters, reserving liquid in a shallow bowl. Separate biscuit dough. Flatten each dough portion slightly and cut into quarters. Place 1 oyster in the center of each dough portion. Wrap dough around oysters, pinching dough edges to form a secure seal. Roll each dough-enclosed oyster in reserved liquid from oysters until well coated, and place on an ungreased baking sheet. Bake for about 5 minutes until golden brown and crisp. Serve hot.

COCKTAIL ROLLUPS

Makes 48

These bite-sized hot appetizers are very popular. You can assemble them ahead of time, cover and refrigerate for up to 2 hours before baking.

2 cans (8 oz. each) refrigerated crescent dinner rolls
1 pkg. (16 oz.) fully cooked smoked cocktail sausages
ketchup and mustard for dipping, optional

Heat oven to 375°. Separate each can of crescent roll dough into 8 triangles. Cut each triangle into 3 triangles of approximately the same size. Place 1 cocktail sausage on the shortest side of each dough triangle and roll up to enclose sausages. Place rollups point-side down on an ungreased baking sheet. Bake for 12 to 15 minutes or until golden brown. Serve warm with ketchup and mustard if desired.

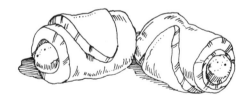

SPICY NACHOS

These are popular as a cocktail snack or prelude to a Mexican-style meal. Look for tortilla chips in a cardboard box, which protects the chips from breaking. You can substitute 1 can (9 oz.) bean dip with jalapeños for refried beans if you have it in the pantry. Spread a thin layer of bean dip on each chip.

1 pkg. (7.5 to 8 oz.) round tortilla chips
1 can (16 oz.) refried beans
1 cup (4 oz.) shredded mozzarella cheese
1 cup (4 oz.) shredded cheddar cheese
1 jar (7-8 oz.) jalapeño pepper nacho slices, drained
1 cup (8 oz. carton) sour cream, optional

Heat oven to 350°. Place chips in a single layer on a large foil-covered baking sheet. Gently spread about 1 tsp. of the beans on each tortilla chip and sprinkle with cheeses. Top each chip with a jalapeño slice. Bake for about 5 minutes, until cheese melts. Slide nachos onto a serving platter and top each nacho with a dollop of sour cream if desired. Serve warm.

VARIATION: MILD NACHOS

Substitute 1 can (4 oz.) chopped green chiles, drained, or 1 can (4.25 oz.) sliced black olives, drained, for jalapeños.

EASY CHEESE WAFERS

Popular at teas or receptions, these are also good served with cocktails, soup or salad. For a pretty presentation, pipe cheese straws from a cookie press fitted with a star tip, following manufacturer's instructions. Form long strips of dough length-wise, 2 inches apart, on ungreased baking sheets. Cut strips into 2-inch straws and bake according to the recipe. Avoid baking these wafers on insulated baking sheets.

1 pkg. (11 oz.) dry pie crust mix
1 jar (5 oz.) Old English sharp pasteurized processed cheese spread
$\frac{1}{4}$ tsp. cayenne pepper, optional

In a medium bowl, mix ingredients together with a fork until well blended. Or, process ingredients with a food processor for about 30 seconds, until mixture forms a ball, stopping often to scrape down the sides. Divide dough in half and shape each half into a 7-x-1$\frac{1}{4}$-inch cylinder. Wrap each cylinder in plastic wrap and refrigerate for 1 hour.

Heat oven to 375°. Unwrap cylinders of dough and cut into $\frac{1}{4}$-inch-wide slices. Place slices on ungreased baking sheets and bake for 8 to 10 minutes, until golden brown. Carefully transfer cheese wafers to wire racks to cool. Store in airtight containers, with waxed paper between each layer.

QUICK CORNISH PASTIES

*Cornish pasties originated in Cornwall, England in the 18th century. Miners would carry them in their pockets for lunch. For a luncheon or supper dish, serve these savory filled pastries with cheese sauce, such as **Cheesy Stroganoff Sauce**, page 132.*

1 can (15 oz.) roast beef hash or corned beef hash
1 can (8.5 oz.) peas and carrots, drained
2 tbs. Worcestershire sauce, optional
2 cans (8 oz. each) refrigerated crescent dinner rolls

Heat oven to 375°. In a medium bowl, combine hash, vegetables and Worcestershire sauce, if using. Place crescent roll dough on a large sheet of waxed paper. Form dough into eight 6-x-3½-inch rectangles by firmly pressing together the diagonal perforations between 8 sets of 2 triangular dough portions. Spread about ¼ cup of the hash mixture on half of each rectangle of dough, leaving a ¼-inch border. Moisten the edges of each rectangle with water and fold unfilled half of rectangle over to enclose filling, lining up the edges. Press edges firmly together with a fork to form a seal. Prick the top of each pasty with fork 3 times. Transfer to an ungreased baking sheet and bake for 13 to 18 minutes or until golden brown. Serve warm.

APPETIZERS, SNACKS AND LIGHT MEALS   39

CHILI TURNOVERS

Serve this family favorite with a tossed salad for lunch or supper.

1 can (15 oz.) chili without beans
2 cans (8 oz. each) refrigerated crescent dinner rolls
$\frac{1}{2}$ cup (2 oz.) shredded sharp cheddar cheese

Heat oven to 375°. Remove any grease from the top of chili. Place crescent roll dough on a large sheet of waxed paper. Form dough into eight 6-x-3½-inch rectangles by firmly pressing together the diagonal perforations between 8 sets of 2 triangular dough portions. Spread about 3 tbs. chili on half of each rectangle, leaving a ¼-inch border. Top chili with 1 tbs. of the cheese. Moisten the edges of each rectangle with water and fold unfilled half of rectangle over to enclose filling, lining up edges. Press edges firmly together with a fork to form a seal. Prick the top of each turnover with a fork 3 times. Transfer turnovers to an ungreased rimmed baking sheet. Bake for 13 to 18 minutes or until golden brown. Serve warm.

FRENCH BREAD PIZZA

*This party favorite is also good served as a light meal. Any of the suggested toppings for **Jiffy Pizzas**, page 42, can be used for variations.*

1 loaf (about 1 lb.) French bread, unsliced
¾ cup pizza sauce
1 pkg. (3.5 oz.) thinly sliced pepperoni (about 50 slices)
1 jar (4.5 oz.) sliced mushrooms, drained
1 can (2.25 oz.) sliced black olives, drained
2 cups (8 oz.) shredded mozzarella cheese

Heat oven to 425°. Slice bread in half horizontally. Place bread halves on an ungreased baking sheet. Spread cut surfaces with pizza sauce. Top each half evenly with pepperoni, mushrooms, olives and cheese. Bake for 12 to 14 minutes, until cheese is melted. Cut into 2-inch slices to serve.

JIFFY PIZZAS

To serve these individual pizza snacks as hot hors d'oeuvres, cut each pizza into 4 wedges with kitchen shears. If you prefer a crisp, rather than chewy, crust, toast the muffins lightly before spooning on the pizza sauce.

6 English muffins, split horizontally
¾ cup pizza sauce
1 cup (4 oz.) shredded mozzarella cheese

Heat oven to 350°. Arrange English muffin halves, cut-side up, on an ungreased baking sheet. Spread each half with 1 tbs. of the pizza sauce and top with 2 to 3 desired toppings (some suggestions follow). Spoon remaining pizza sauce evenly over toppings. Sprinkle cheese evenly over pizzas. Bake for 12 to 15 minutes, until cheese melts. Serve hot.

TOPPINGS

- 1 pkg. (2 oz.) anchovy fillets, drained, cut into pieces
- 1 can (3.75 oz.) sardines, drained, cut into pieces
- 1 can (4 oz.) chopped green chiles, drained
- 1 can (2 oz.) sliced mushrooms, drained
- 1 can (2.25 oz.) sliced black olives, drained
- 1 pkg. (3.5 oz.) thinly sliced pepperoni (about 50 slices)
- 1 pkg. (7 oz.) fully cooked brown-and-serve sausage links, sliced

VARIATION: JIFFY MEXICAN PIZZAS

Substitute 1 can (10 oz.) mild enchilada sauce for pizza sauce. Top pizzas with chopped green chiles, sliced black olives and sliced sausage links. Substitute cheddar cheese for mozzarella.

EASY CHEESE FONDUE

Servings: 18 as an appetizer; 4 as a light meal

This simplified version of a classic is a favorite dish for company, as it makes an appealing appetizer, or can solo as the whole meal. It is not necessary to include a crust on each bread cube if cubes are cut several hours ahead of time and allowed to dry. If the fondue becomes too thick or stringy, stir in ¼ to ½ cup dry white wine, beer or cider. Leftover fondue is good reheated and served over toast or vegetables. For variety, serve at least three of the dippers with the fondue.

2 cans (10.75 oz. each) condensed cheddar cheese soup
1 cup (4 oz.) finely shredded Swiss cheese
assorted *Dippers*

DIPPERS

- canned quartered artichoke hearts, well drained
- canned button mushrooms, drained
- canned pitted black olives, drained
- luncheon meat, cubed
- Vienna sausages or wieners, cut into bite-sized pieces
- breadstick pieces

- French, Italian, or rye bread, cut into 1-inch cubes, each with some crust
- frozen waffles, toasted and cubed
- frozen fried potato nuggets, baked
- spoon-sized shredded wheat cereal
- small fresh mushrooms
- cherry tomatoes

In an electric fondue pot, heavy 1-quart saucepan or the top of a double boiler over simmering water, stir soup until smooth and add cheese. Cook over medium heat until cheese melts, stirring constantly. Serve in electric fondue pot or transfer to a chafing dish, casserole or ceramic fondue pot over a heating element. Keep warm over low heat.

VARIATION: ONION CHEDDAR FONDUE

Replace 1 can of the soup with 1 cup (8 oz. carton) refrigerated French onion dip. Substitute shredded sharp cheddar cheese for Swiss cheese.

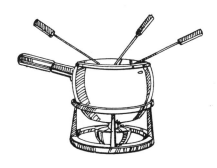

EMERGENCY SANDWICHES

Keep these ingredients on hand, as these hot, open-faced sandwiches can be a real lifesaver. To halve the recipe, use 1 can of the soup and one 6-ounce can tuna.

6 English muffins, split horizontally
2 cans (10.75 oz. each) condensed cheddar cheese soup
1 can (12 oz.) chunk light tuna, drained, broken into chunks

Heat broiler. Place English muffin halves on a baking sheet, cut-side up. Toast lightly under broiler, taking care that muffins do not burn. In a medium bowl, mix soup with tuna chunks. Spread mixture evenly on toasted English muffin halves. Broil sandwiches for 5 minutes or until hot and bubbly.

SOUPS AND SALADS

SIMPLE SOUPS

Substantial and nutritious soups, chowders and bisques can be made from convenience products with delicious results. With a little creativity, they practically make themselves. Experiment with different combinations of products to make your own customized recipe.

- Start with canned chicken, beef or vegetable broth and condensed soup. Bottled clam juice makes a good foundation for seafood-based soups.
- Canned and packaged vegetables, beans, chicken, and seafood contribute color, flavor and fiber.
- To cut the salt content, use reduced-sodium soups and rinse canned beans with water several times before adding to soup mixture.
- To enrich convenience soups with additional vitamins and minerals, replace part of the liquid in a recipe with leftover chicken or meat juices, or the liquid in which vegetables are packed or cooked.
- When serving soup as an appetizer, allow $1/2$ to $3/4$ cup per person. When serving as a main dish, allow 1 to $1 1/2$ cups per serving.

ONION SOUP

This makes a perfect beginning to a meal or an easy Sunday supper treat. No butter is needed to sauté the onions. As they thaw, they cook in their own water.

1 pkg. (12 oz.) frozen chopped onions
1 can (10.75 oz.) condensed beef broth
1 can (10.75 oz.) condensed beef consommé
grated Parmesan cheese for garnish

In a 2-quart saucepan, cook onions over medium-low heat for 15 minutes, stirring occasionally. Add broth and consommé and bring mixture to a boil. Reduce heat to low, cover and simmer for about 15 minutes. Pass Parmesan cheese to garnish each serving.

VARIATION: FRENCH ONION SOUP

Place ½ slice of toasted French bread in each of 4 small soup bowls and pour hot soup over bread. Sprinkle generously with Parmesan cheese and serve immediately.

CREAMY POTATO SOUP

Here's a simple way to prepare a really tasty soup.

1 pkg. (24-26 oz.) frozen shredded hash brown potatoes
1½ cups frozen chopped onions
2 cans (10.75 oz. each) condensed chicken broth
2⅔ cups (2 soup cans) water
1 can (10.75 oz.) condensed cream of celery soup
1 can (10.75 oz.) condensed cream of chicken soup
2 cups milk
shredded cheddar cheese for garnish, optional

Combine potatoes, onions, chicken broth and water in a Dutch oven or large saucepan and bring to a boil. Stir occasionally to separate potatoes. Reduce heat to low, cover and simmer for 30 minutes, stirring occasionally. Stir soup in cans and add to potato mixture with milk. Heat through, but do not boil, stirring occasionally. Garnish each serving with shredded cheese if desired.

CREAMY CAULIFLOWER SOUP

Frozen cauliflower is the secret to this quick homemade soup.

1 pkg. (8 oz.) frozen cauliflower
½ cup water
2 cans (10.75 oz. each) cream of potato soup
2 cups milk
1 cup (4 oz.) shredded Swiss cheese

Combine cauliflower and water in a 3-quart saucepan or Dutch oven. Bring to a boil over high heat. Reduce heat to low, cover and simmer for 5 minutes, until cauliflower is tender, stirring once. Mash cauliflower slightly with a fork or potato masher, cutting up large pieces if necessary. Stir soup in cans and add to cauliflower mixture. Stir in milk and cheese. Heat through, stirring, but do not boil.

SPEEDY PINTO BEAN SOUP

Serve with a green salad and some tortilla chips for a quick lunch or supper. Use regular, spicy or vegetarian beans.

1 can (28 oz.) crushed tomatoes
1½ cups frozen chopped onions
1 can (30 oz.) refried beans
1 can (14.5 oz.) chicken broth
shredded Monterey Jack cheese for garnish, optional

In a 3-quart saucepan or Dutch oven, combine tomatoes and onions. Bring to a boil over high heat and boil for 5 minutes, stirring occasionally. Stir in beans and broth. Reduce heat to low and simmer for 15 minutes, stirring occasionally. Garnish each serving with shredded cheese if desired.

VARIATION: SPEEDY BLACK BEAN SOUP

Substitute 2 cans (16 oz. each) refried black beans for refried beans.

SOUTHWESTERN SOUP

Servings: 4

This soup will beat the chill in less than 20 minutes.

1 can (15 oz.) black beans, rinsed and drained
1 can (14.5 oz.) golden hominy, rinsed and drained
1 can (14.5 oz.) Mexican-style stewed tomatoes
1 can (14.5 oz.) chicken broth
chopped fresh cilantro for garnish, optional

In a 3-quart saucepan or Dutch oven, combine all ingredients. Bring to a boil over high heat. Reduce heat to low and simmer, stirring occasionally, until heated through. Garnish each serving with chopped cilantro if desired.

MINUTE MINESTRONE

This hearty main-dish Italian vegetable soup has "from-scratch" flavor. Serve with hot crusty garlic bread or Italian breadsticks.

1 pkg. (1.4 oz.) dry vegetable soup mix
1 can (14.5 oz.) Italian-style stewed tomatoes
1 pkg. (10 oz.) frozen mixed vegetables
4 cups water
1 pkg. (10 oz.) frozen chopped spinach, optional
1 can (15 oz.) kidney beans, rinsed and drained, or New Orleans-style red beans
grated Parmesan cheese for garnish

In a 3-quart saucepan or Dutch oven, blend together soup mix, tomatoes, mixed vegetables and water. Add spinach if desired. Bring to a boil over high heat, stirring occasionally to break up vegetables. Reduce heat to low and stir in kidney beans. Cover and simmer for 15 minutes, stirring occasionally, until heated through. Garnish each serving with Parmesan cheese.

TORTELLINI-VEGETABLE SOUP

Here's a delicious new version of chicken noodle soup. If desired, you can substitute 2 cups cubed leftover chicken for packaged chicken.

2 cans (14.5 oz. each) chicken broth
1 pkg. (9 oz.) refrigerated cheese-stuffed
   tortellini
1 pkg. (21 oz.) teriyaki stir-fry vegetables
   with teriyaki sauce
1 pkg. (9 oz.) frozen diced cooked
chicken, or 1 can (10 oz.) chunk white
   chicken, broken into chunks

Combine chicken broth and tortellini in a 3-quart saucepan or Dutch oven. Bring to a boil over high heat. Add vegetables and sauce and return mixture to a boil. Reduce heat to medium and cook, covered, for 5 minutes. Stir in chicken and heat for 5 minutes.

COLD WEATHER SOUP

Pack this popular soup in a vacuum bottle for a tailgate party.

1 can (10.75 oz.) condensed cheddar
   cheese soup
1 can (10.75 oz.) condensed chili beef
   soup with beans
1 can (10.75 oz.) condensed tomato soup
$3\frac{1}{3}$ cups ($2\frac{1}{2}$ soup cans) water

In a 3-quart saucepan or Dutch oven, combine soups, stirring until well blended. Gradually stir in water and heat over medium heat, stirring often, until mixture just comes to a boil. Reduce heat to low and simmer for about 15 minutes, stirring occasionally.

MEXICAN BEEF AND VEGETABLE SOUP

For a real treat, serve this hearty soup topped with shredded cheddar cheese and crushed corn chips.

1 lb. lean ground beef
1 pkg. (1.25-1.5 oz.) dry taco seasoning mix
1 can (8 oz.) tomato sauce
1 can (15.25 oz.) whole kernel golden corn
1 can (15 oz.) kidney beans, rinsed and drained
1 can (14.5 oz.) Mexican-style stewed tomatoes
1 cup water

In a 3-quart saucepan or Dutch oven, cook ground beef over medium heat until browned, stirring to break apart. Drain well on paper towels and return to skillet. Add remaining ingredients and bring mixture to a boil. Reduce heat to low and simmer uncovered for 10 minutes until heated through.

CHILI CON CARNE

This combination of convenience foods has real Mexican flavor. Serve this chili with saltine crackers or corn chips, or over hot cooked rice. To dress up the chili for company, place chopped avocados, green chiles, onion, tomato and sliced black olives in individual bowls. Let your guests sprinkle their choice of toppings over their portions of chili.

1 can (15 oz.) chili without beans
1 can (15.5 oz.) chili beans
1 can (14.5 oz.) Mexican-style stewed tomatoes
1 can (8-8.75 oz.) whole kernel golden corn, drained
1 cup (4 oz.) shredded sharp cheddar cheese

Remove any grease from the top of chili. In a 2-quart saucepan, combine chili, beans, tomatoes and corn. Cover and simmer over medium heat, stirring often, until heated through. Garnish each serving with shredded cheese.

SAUSAGE VEGETABLE SOUP

This chunky soup makes a good lunch served with hot buttered cornbread.

1 pkg. (7 oz.) frozen cooked brown-and-serve sausage links
1 can (10.75 oz.) condensed green pea soup
1 can (10.75 oz.) condensed old-fashioned vegetable soup
2⅔ cups (2 soup cans) water

In a 3-quart saucepan or Dutch oven, brown sausages according to package directions. With the tip of a spoon, cut sausages into thirds. Add soups and stir until well blended. Slowly stir in water and simmer over medium heat, stirring often, until heated through.

VARIATION: SAUSAGE MINESTRONE

Substitute 2 cans (10.75 oz. each) condensed minestrone soup for green pea and vegetable soups. Garnish each serving with a dollop of prepared pesto if desired.

CREAMY CLAM AND MUSHROOM SOUP

For a touch of color, garnish this tasty soup with thin lemon slices and snipped parsley.

1 can (10.75 oz.) condensed cream of
　　mushroom soup
1 bottle (8 oz.) clam juice
1 can (6.5 oz.) chopped clams in clam juice

In a 1-quart saucepan, combine soup with clam juice and stir until well mixed. Add clams with juice. Simmer over low heat until heated through, stirring occasionally.

VARIATION: VEGETABLE SOUP WITH CLAMS

Substitute 1 can (10.75 oz.) condensed vegetarian vegetable soup for cream of mushroom soup.

CLAM CHOWDER

This variation of a family favorite tastes like it is homemade.

2 cans (10.75 oz. each) condensed New England clam chowder
1⅓ cups (1 soup can) water
1 can (11 oz.) whole kernel golden corn
2 cups half-and-half or milk
1 pkg. (1 oz.) dry onion soup mix
chopped fresh parsley for garnish, optional

In a 3-quart saucepan or Dutch oven, combine all ingredients and stir until well blended. Over medium heat, heat mixture until it just boils, stirring constantly. Reduce heat to low and simmer for 10 minutes, stirring often. Garnish with chopped parsley if desired.

CREAMY CRAB BISQUE

Rich-tasting, and elegant enough to serve for a special occasion, this bisque can be served hot or chilled. For a different flavor, you can substitute 1 can (10.75 oz.) condensed cream of asparagus soup for the pea soup. If you don't have half-and-half, you can use 1 can (5 oz.) evaporated milk plus 1 can of water.

1 can (10.75 oz.) condensed green pea soup
1 can (10.75 oz.) condensed tomato bisque or tomato soup
2 cups half-and-half
1 can (6 oz.) crabmeat, drained
2 tbs. dry sherry, or to taste, optional
chopped fresh parsley for garnish, optional
thin lemon slices for garnish, optional

In a 2-quart saucepan, combine soups and stir until well blended. Gradually add half-and-half to soup mixture, stirring until smooth. Heat over low heat until heated through, but do not boil. Stir occasionally. Add crabmeat and heat through gently. Stir in sherry if desired. Garnish each portion with parsley if desired.

To serve chilled, cool bisque to room temperature. Cover and refrigerate for 3 to 4 hours until well chilled. Stir well and serve in chilled soup bowls, garnished with thin lemon slices.

SWIFT SALADS

The versatile salad adds color, flavor and diversity to a meal. It can be served as a snack, first course, side dish or main course. Some salads can even double as dessert. The following ideas are great for busy cooks. Or, make up your own.

- Combine packaged, rinsed and trimmed fresh spinach, torn into bite-size pieces, with well-drained Mandarin orange segments and bottled vinaigrette dressing.
- Toss packaged cole slaw mix with creamy bottled dressing or *Orange Mayonnaise Sauce*, page 145. Sliced stuffed olives, sliced pimientos or canned green peas can be added for color. Refrigerate until serving time.
- Top drained canned fruit cocktail with cottage cheese, sour cream, yogurt, *Creamy Fresh Fruit Sauce*, page 144 , or *Lemon Cream Sauce*, page 145.
- Just before serving, combine packaged mixed salad greens with one or more of the following canned or packaged items (remember to drain or rinse items if necessary): marinated artichoke hearts or mushrooms; sliced hearts of palm; sliced water chestnuts; canned crabmeat or shrimp; crumbled or shredded cheeses; bottled bacon bits; salted nut pieces; broken corn chips; garbanzo or kidney beans; shoestring potato sticks; French fried onion rings; smoked oysters; bean sprouts; cubed luncheon meat; croutons or stuffing mix cubes; Mandarin orange segments; whole or sliced olives; chopped pimientos; sliced pepperoncini (Greek salad peppers).

CORN AND BEAN MEDLEY

Servings: 8

This marinated deli-style salad adds color and texture to your meal. Look for a bottled vinaigrette salad dressing made with red wine vinegar and olive oil.

1 can (15 oz.) garbanzo beans, rinsed and drained
1 can (15 oz.) kidney beans, rinsed and drained
1 can (11 oz.) golden corn with red and green peppers, drained
1/2 cup vinaigrette salad dressing

Toss ingredients together in a medium bowl.

THREE BEAN SALAD

This popular dish is great for picnics and cookouts. It will keep for several days, tightly covered, in the refrigerator. For a main dish for 6, spoon this salad onto lettuce-lined dinner plates. Drain 3 chilled 6-ounce cans of chunk light tuna and break tuna into bite-sized chunks. Surround each serving of salad with tuna chunks and garnish with lemon wedges and chopped scallions.

1 can (14.5 oz.) cut green beans, rinsed and drained
1 can (15 oz.) red kidney beans, rinsed and drained
1 can (15 oz.) garbanzo beans, rinsed and drained
1 jar (4 oz.) sliced pimientos, rinsed and drained
1 cup (8 oz. bottle) Italian salad dressing

Toss all ingredients together in a large bowl. Cover and marinate in the refrigerator for at least 4 hours or overnight. Before serving, toss ingredients together. Serve with a slotted spoon.

VARIATION: MARINATED BEANS AND ARTICHOKE HEARTS   Servings: 6

Substitute 1 can (13.75 oz.) quartered artichoke hearts, drained, for kidney beans; substitute 1 can (14.5 oz.) cut yellow wax beans, drained, for garbanzo beans.

MARINATED VEGETABLE SALAD

This is wonderful for a buffet supper. For real homemade flavor, add 1 to 2 thinly sliced medium onions. This salad will keep for several days, tightly covered, in the refrigerator.

2 cans (14.5 oz. each) green peas and diced carrots, well drained
1 can (15 oz.) cut or sliced beets, well drained
1 can (14.5 oz.) cut green beans, well drained
1 cup (8 oz. bottle) Italian salad dressing

In a large bowl, combine all ingredients. Toss lightly until vegetables are well coated. Cover and marinate in the refrigerator for at least 4 hours or overnight. Toss ingredients together before serving. Serve with a slotted spoon.

PASTA PRIMAVERA SALAD

For an economical European-style country supper, serve this salad with a variety of cold cuts and warm crusty rolls. This salad holds well and is ideal for packing in a cooler for picnics. Any type of unfilled pasta will work, from small shell macaroni to fettuccine.

1 pkg. (16 oz.) dry pasta
1 pkg. (16 oz.) frozen broccoli, carrots, water chestnuts and red peppers
1 cup (8 oz. bottle) Italian salad dressing
grated Parmesan cheese for garnish, optional

Cook pasta according to package directions, rinse in cold water and drain well. Place drained pasta in a large bowl. Run cold water over vegetables in a colander to thaw completely; drain well. Add vegetables and salad dressing to pasta and toss lightly. Cover and refrigerate for at least 1 hour before serving. Garnish with grated Parmesan cheese if desired.

MACARONI-TUNA SALAD

For an attractive luncheon dish, fill tomato cups with this salad and place on lettuce-lined plates with hot corn muffins. To make tomato cups, cut 5 or 6 chilled medium tomatoes into sixths beginning at the center of stem end, but do not cut all the way through. Leave $1/2$ inch of the tomato uncut at the base. Spread the segments apart and sprinkle the inside lightly with salt. Fill the center of tomatoes with salad.

1 can (14.75-15 oz.) macaroni and cheese
1 can (6 oz.) chunk light tuna, drained, broken into chunks
1 can (8.5 oz.) young sweet peas, drained
$1/2$ cup mayonnaise

Combine ingredients in a medium bowl and mix well. Cover and refrigerate for at least 1 hour, until well chilled.

TACO SALAD

This hearty salad makes a great main dish. It's tasty, economical and quick to prepare.

1 lb. ground turkey or lean ground beef
1 pkg. (1.25-1.5 oz.) dry taco seasoning mix
¾ cup water
8 cups mixed salad greens, torn into bite-sized pieces
1 jar (8 oz.) thick and chunky salsa
1 can (2.25 oz.) sliced black olives, drained
1 pkg. (10.5 oz.) corn chips
1 cup (4 oz.) shredded sharp cheddar cheese

In a 10-inch nonstick skillet, cook turkey over medium-high heat until browned, stirring to break apart. Drain well on paper towels and return to skillet. Stir in seasoning mix and water. Simmer over low heat, uncovered, for 10 minutes, stirring occasionally.

In a large bowl, toss together lettuce, salsa and olive slices. On each of 4 plates, layer ¼ of the corn chips, ¼ of the lettuce mixture and ¼ of the turkey mixture. Top each serving with ¼ cup of the shredded cheese.

CRANBERRY RELISH SALAD

Serve this tangy salad with roast chicken, turkey or ham. Serve on lettuce-lined plates and top salad with mayonnaise if desired. You can substitute cherry-, orange- or orange-pineapple-flavored gelatin for the raspberry-flavored gelatin if desired. For cranberry sauce, you can substitute 1 jar (15 oz.) applesauce.

1 cup boiling water
1 pkg. (6 oz.) raspberry-flavored gelatin
1 can (16 oz.) whole berry cranberry sauce
1 can (8 oz.) crushed pineapple

Pour boiling water over gelatin in an 8-inch square baking dish, stirring for about 2 minutes, until gelatin is dissolved. Immediately add cranberry sauce and stir until smooth. Stir in undrained pineapple. Chill until firm.

CREAMY FRUIT SALAD

Buttermilk is the surprise ingredient in this appealing salad. Be sure to set your kitchen timer so that you will remember to stir the salad at the appropriate time.

1 can (20 oz.) crushed pineapple with juice
1 pkg. (6 oz.) peach-, orange-, raspberry- or strawberry-flavored gelatin
2 cups (1 pt.) buttermilk
1 pkg. (8 oz.) frozen whipped dessert topping, thawed
lettuce leaves for garnish, optional

In a 3-quart saucepan, bring pineapple and juice to a boil; remove from heat. Stir gelatin into pineapple mixture until dissolved; cool. Blend buttermilk and whipped topping into cooled pineapple mixture and spread in a 9-x-13-x-2-inch glass dish. Chill mixture for 45 minutes. Stir well and chill until firm. Serve on lettuce-lined salad plates if desired.

FAST FRUIT CUP

Add vitamin C to your meal as well as eye-appeal with this tasty fruit salad. For real homemade flavor and appearance, stir in ½ cup chopped unpeeled apples, sliced bananas or a combination of both.

1 can (30 oz.) fruit cocktail, chilled, well drained
1⅓ cups (3.5 oz. can) flaked coconut
1 can (6 oz.) frozen orange juice concentrate, partially thawed

In a large bowl, toss fruit cocktail and coconut with orange juice concentrate. Serve immediately in small bowls or sherbet glasses.

SIDE DISHES AND SPECIAL BREADS

ASPARAGUS CASSEROLE

This goes well with a sliced ham dinner. If desired, stir 3 to 4 chopped hard-cooked eggs into the mixture before baking.

1 can (10.75 oz.) condensed cheddar cheese soup
2 cans (14.5 oz. each) cut green asparagus, drained
1 can (2.8 oz.) French fried onions

Heat oven to 350°. In a 1½-quart shallow baking dish, gently mix soup with asparagus. Bake uncovered for 25 minutes or until hot and bubbly. Sprinkle with onions and bake for 5 additional minutes.

SPINACH CASSEROLE

*Even spinach-haters like this dish, which can be prepared the day before, covered and refrigerated until ready to bake. For a luncheon dish, arrange 2 or 3 sliced hard-cooked eggs on the baked casserole. Return it to the oven for 2 additional minutes. To thaw spinach quickly, refer to **Tips for Frozen Foods**, page 6.*

2 pkg. (10 oz. each) frozen chopped spinach, thawed, well drained
1 can (10.75 oz.) condensed cream of mushroom soup
1 cup (4 oz.) shredded sharp cheddar cheese
$\frac{1}{2}$ cup (2.5 oz. jar) sliced mushrooms, drained

Heat oven to 350°. In a $1\frac{1}{2}$-quart casserole, combine spinach, soup, $\frac{1}{2}$ cup of the cheese and mushrooms; mix well. Top mixture with remaining cheese. Bake uncovered for 20 to 25 minutes, until mixture is hot and bubbly.

VARIATION: SPINACH TOMATO CASSEROLE

Substitute 1 cup (8 oz. carton) sour cream and 1 can (8 oz.) tomato sauce for mushroom soup.

SPICY GREEN BEANS

Surprise! A dry seasoning mix contributes interesting flavor to this colorful casserole. Be sure that the casserole you choose can be used on the stovetop as well as in the oven.

1 pkg. (1.5 oz.) dry Sloppy Joe seasoning mix
1 can (6 oz.) tomato paste
1 cup water
2 cans (14.5 oz. each) French-style green beans, drained
1 cup (4 oz.) shredded sharp cheddar cheese

Heat oven to 350°. In a 1½-quart ceramic casserole or pyrex saucepan, combine seasoning mix with tomato paste and water. Bring to a boil, stirring constantly until thickened. Remove from heat. Add green beans and mix well. Sprinkle with cheese. Bake uncovered for 20 minutes or until beans are heated through and cheese is golden brown.

PINEAPPLE-BEAN BAKE

Pineapple adds zest to this tasty side dish. It can also serve 6 as a light meal.

2 cans (16 oz. each) pork and beans in tomato sauce
1 can (15.25 oz.) pineapple chunks, drained
1 can (12 oz.) luncheon meat, cut crosswise into 8-10 slices

Heat oven to 350°. In a 1½-quart casserole, gently mix pork and beans with pineapple. Arrange meat slices on top of mixture, overlapping slightly. Bake uncovered for 30 minutes or until hot and bubbly.

THREE-CORN DELIGHT

Three types of crisp corn and an easy cream sauce make a truly delightful dish.

1 can (11 oz.) golden corn
1 can (11 oz.) white corn
1 can (11 oz.) golden corn with red and green peppers
1 pkg. (8 oz.) cream cheese

Drain corn, reserving ¼ cup of the liquid. In a 2-quart saucepan, combine reserved corn liquid and cream cheese, cutting cream cheese into pieces with the side of a spoon. Cook mixture over medium heat, stirring constantly until smooth. Reduce heat to low. Add corn, stirring until evenly coated and heated through.

MEXICAN HOMINY CASSEROLE

Servings: 6-8

Green chiles and cheese turn hominy into an adventurous side dish. It's great for breakfast or brunch.

2 cups (8 oz.) shredded sharp cheddar cheese
1 can (29 oz.) white hominy, drained
1 can (4-5 oz.) chopped green chiles, drained
1 cup (8 oz. carton) sour cream

Heat oven to 350°. In a lightly greased 2-quart casserole, combine 1 cup of the cheese with remaining ingredients; mix well. Bake for about 20 minutes, until hot and bubbly. Sprinkle with remaining cheese and bake for 5 additional minutes.

POTATOES IN CREAM

If desired, sprinkle the baked casserole with shredded cheddar cheese and return it to the oven until cheese melts.

1 pkg. (12 oz.) frozen shredded hash brown potato patties, thawed, or 2 cups
    frozen shredded hash brown potatoes
salt and pepper to taste
1 cup (½ pt.) heavy whipping cream

Heat oven to 350°. Place hash brown potatoes in a greased 1-quart shallow casserole, crumbling patties if necessary. Sprinkle with salt and pepper. Cover with cream. Bake uncovered for about 1 hour, until potato edges are lightly browned.

CHEESY POTATO BAKE

Serve this easy casserole with fried sausage or ham and tomatoes for a weekend breakfast or brunch.

1 pkg. (12 oz.) frozen shredded hash brown potato patties, thawed, or 2 cups
   frozen shredded hash brown potatoes
1 can (10.75 oz.) condensed cream of potato or cream of mushroom soup
1 cup (8 oz. carton) sour cream
1 cup (4 oz.) shredded sharp cheddar cheese
½ cup grated Parmesan cheese

Heat oven to 350°. Place hash brown potatoes in a medium bowl, crumbling portions if necessary. Add remaining ingredients and mix well. Spoon mixture into a lightly greased 1½-quart shallow baking dish and cover with aluminum foil. Bake for 25 minutes. Uncover and bake for about 15 minutes, until golden brown.

CHILES STUFFED WITH RICE

Include this in your next Mexican dinner menu. If desired, you can substitute 1 can (16 oz.) refried beans for Spanish rice.

1 cans (7 oz.) whole roasted green chiles, drained
1 can (15 oz.) Spanish rice
½ cup (2 oz.) shredded sharp cheddar cheese

Heat oven to 350°. Make a lengthwise slit in each chile with the top of a sharp knife and place in a lightly greased 8-inch square baking dish. Fill chiles with equal portions of rice and sprinkle with cheese. Bake uncovered for 15 to 20 minutes until rice is heated through and cheese is melted.

SPANISH RICE AND BEANS

This double-quick dish is a tasty time-saver. Serve it over crisp corn chips if desired. Look for canned Spanish rice in the Mexican foods section or near the canned chili in the supermarket. You can give this dish an Italian spin by substituting 1 can (14.75 oz.) spaghetti in tomato sauce with cheese for Spanish rice.

1 can (15 oz.) chili with beans
1 can (15 oz.) Spanish rice
$\frac{1}{2}$ cup (2 oz.) shredded sharp cheddar cheese

Remove any grease from the top of chili. In a 2-quart saucepan, combine chili with Spanish rice. Simmer over low heat until heated through, stirring gently once or twice. Sprinkle each serving with a small amount of cheese.

MINUTE MACARONI AND CHEESE

Servings: 4-6

Add zip to this popular side dish by stirring in a few drops of Worcestershire sauce, or 1 tbs. prepared mustard. If desired, you can substitute 1 jar (8 oz.) pasteurized processed cheese sauce for the cheese soup.

2 cups (7-8 oz. pkg.) elbow macaroni
1 can (10.75 oz.) condensed cheddar cheese soup

Heat oven to 400°. Cook macaroni according to package directions; drain and immediately place in a lightly greased 1½-quart casserole. Add soup and toss gently until well mixed. Bake uncovered for about 15 minutes, or until heated through.

VARIATION: "WEENIE" MACARONI AND CHEESE

Servings: 6

Add 1 pkg. (12-14 oz.) frankfurters, cut into ½-inch pieces. Use a 3-quart casserole.

FETTUCCINE ALFREDO

You can also serve this rich, delicious classic as an appetizer or main course.

1 pkg. (12 oz.) medium egg noodles
1/2 cup (1 stick) butter
1 cup (1/2 pt.) heavy whipping cream
3/4 cup (3 oz.) grated Parmesan cheese
salt to taste
white pepper to taste, optional

Cook noodles according to package directions until tender but slightly firm in the center (*al dente*). While noodles are cooking, melt butter over low heat in a 1-quart saucepan, taking care not to let it brown. Stir in cream and warm slightly. Stir in cheese, salt and white pepper, if using. Keep mixture warm over the lowest possible heat. Place well-drained, hot cooked noodles in a warm serving dish. Pour cheese sauce over noodles and toss gently with a large fork and spoon until well coated. Serve immediately.

BUTTER ROLLS

It's easy to turn a can of biscuits into delicious dinner rolls.

½ cup (1 stick) butter
1 can (10 oz.) refrigerated large-sized buttermilk biscuits
poppy or sesame seeds, optional

Heat oven to 400°. Melt butter in a 9-x-13-inch baking pan. Separate biscuit dough and cut each dough portion in half. Roll each dough half between your palms to form a ball. Roll each ball in melted butter until well coated. Arrange balls in pan in 5 rows of 4 balls each. Sprinkle with seeds if desired. Bake for 10 minutes or until golden brown. Remove rolls from oven and let sit in pan until any remaining butter has been absorbed. Serve warm.

FANCY CRESCENT ROLLS

Makes 8

These tasty rolls are really versatile. Serve the sweet version for breakfast or as a snack. Serve the savory versions as hors d'oeuvres, with your main meal or with eggs, soup or salad.

1 can (8 oz.) refrigerated crescent dinner rolls
½ cup ready-to-use almond cake and pastry filling, or 1 can (4.25 oz.) deviled ham
    spread, or ½ cup (4 oz.) shredded cheddar cheese

Heat oven to 375°. Separate crescent roll dough into 8 triangles. Spread about 1 tbs. of desired filling over each dough portion. Starting at the shortest side of triangles, roll up dough portions to enclose filling, ending at the opposite point. Place rolls, point-side down, on an ungreased baking sheet and curve ends to form a crescent shape. Bake for 10 to 13 minutes, until golden brown. Cool for 5 minutes on a wire rack. Serve warm.

COMPANY BREAD RING

This attractive bread is easy to make and inexpensive. Any leftover slices can be wrapped in aluminum foil and reheated the next day.

$\frac{1}{2}$ cup (1 stick) butter
3 cans (12 oz. each) refrigerated flaky buttermilk biscuits

Heat oven to 350°. Melt butter in a nonstick Bundt pan or ring mold in the oven. Remove biscuit dough from cans but do not separate. Place biscuit dough on its side in pan. Press biscuit dough portions together to form a continuous circle. Bake for 25 to 30 minutes, until golden brown. Let bread sit in pan briefly until remaining butter has been absorbed. Invert onto a serving plate. Serve hot.

PARTY BREAD

To save time and electricity, put 1 or 2 of these loaves into the oven during the last 25 minutes of cooking time when you are baking dishes at 350°. If you are barbecuing, place foil-wrapped loaves on the grill with your meat or vegetables for 15 to 20 minutes or until heated through. The loaves can be wrapped securely in foil and frozen for several weeks. To serve, defrost for 30 minutes and bake as directed. Use soft French bread loaves that are approximately 14 to 15 inches long and about 5 inches wide.

2 loaves (about 1 lb. each) French or Italian bread, unsliced
Seasoned Butter Spread, page 141

Heat oven to 350°. With a sharp knife, slice loaves of bread in half lengthwise. Slice each half diagonally at 1-inch intervals, cutting to, but not through, bottom crust. Spread *Seasoned Butter Spread* between slices and over tops. Reassemble loaves and wrap each in heavy-duty aluminum foil. Bake for 15 minutes. Open tops of foil and bake for 5 to 10 minutes. To serve, fold foil edges down to form a basket. Break off bread slices as needed.

TOASTED CHEESE BREAD

Servings: 28-30

Serve this crusty treat at your next cookout or as an accompaniment to soup or salad. Look for soft French bread loaves that are approximately 14 to 15 inches long and about 5 inches wide.

1 cup (2 sticks) softened butter or margarine
¾ cup (3 oz.) grated Parmesan cheese, or 2 pkg. (1.25-1.5 oz. each) dry cheese
   sauce mix
2 loaves (about 1 lb. each) French or Italian bread, unsliced

Heat oven to 400°. Combine butter and cheese in a small bowl until well blended; set aside. With a sharp knife, slice loaves of bread in half lengthwise. Slice each half diagonally at 1-inch intervals, cutting to, but not through, bottom crust. Spread butter mixture between slices and over tops. Place loaves on an ungreased baking sheet and bake for 5 to 10 minutes or until golden brown. Serve immediately.

ORANGE-COCONUT TEA RING

Out of a can of sweet rolls comes a "homemade" tea ring.

2 cans (13.9 oz. each) refrigerated orange Danish sweet rolls with icing
$\frac{1}{2}$ cup flaked coconut

Heat oven to 400°. Separate sweet roll dough into disks. Arrange half of the dough disks around the bottom of a greased $6\frac{1}{2}$-cup ring mold or Bundt pan, topping-side up. Arrange remaining rolls on top, covering the seams of rolls on bottom layer. Bake for about 20 minutes, until tea ring is golden brown. Cool briefly in mold on a wire cake rack. Invert tea ring onto a serving plate. Immediately spread the top and sides with icing and sprinkle with coconut. Serve warm.

VARIATION: CINNAMON-NUT TEA RING

Substitute 1 can (12.4 oz.) refrigerated cinnamon rolls with icing for orange Danish sweet rolls. Substitute $\frac{1}{4}$ cup chopped pecans or walnuts for coconut.

MAIN DISH CASSEROLES

BAKED RAVIOLI-BROCCOLI CASSEROLE

Servings: 4-6

*This appealing dinner is ready to serve in 30 minutes. To thaw frozen broccoli quickly, refer to **Tips for Frozen Foods,** page 6.*

1 cup (8 oz. carton) sour cream
2 can (15 oz. each) beef ravioli
1 pkg. (10 oz.) frozen chopped broccoli, thawed
1 cup (4 oz.) shredded mozzarella cheese

Heat oven to 375°. In a large bowl, gently mix sour cream with beef ravioli and broccoli. Spread mixture in a lightly greased 3-quart shallow baking dish. Sprinkle evenly with mozzarella cheese. Bake uncovered for about 25 minutes until heated through.

CHICKEN MACARONI CASSEROLE

Servings: 4-5

Dress up canned macaroni and cheese for a quick, tasty meal. If desired, you can substitute 1 can (6 oz.) chunk light tuna, drained and broken into chunks, for the chicken.

1 can (3 oz.) chow mein noodles
1 can (10.75) oz. condensed cream of chicken soup
1 can (5 oz.) chunk white chicken, drained, broken into chunks
1 can (14.75-15 oz.) macaroni and cheese
1-2 tbs. canned chopped green chiles, optional

Heat oven to 350°. In a 2-quart casserole, combine ½ of the chow mein noodles with soup, chicken chunks, macaroni and cheese and chiles, if using. Bake uncovered for about 25 minutes or until hot and bubbly. Sprinkle remaining noodles around the edge of casserole and bake for 5 additional minutes.

CHICKEN TORTILLA CASSEROLE

South-of-the-border ingredients are combined with chicken for a hearty make-ahead dish. This dish works well with leftover chicken or turkey. Or, use 1 pkg. (9 oz.) frozen diced cooked chicken.

1 can (10.75 oz.) condensed creamy chicken mushroom soup
1 can (5 oz.) evaporated milk
2 cups cooked chicken or turkey, cubed
1 can (4 oz.) chopped green chiles, drained
6 corn tortillas, torn into bite-sized pieces, or $1\frac{1}{2}$ cups coarsely crumbled
   tortilla chips
1 cup (4 oz.) shredded cheddar cheese

In a medium bowl, blend soup with evaporated milk; stir in chicken and chopped green chiles. Cover the bottom of a lightly greased 8-inch square baking dish with $\frac{1}{2}$ of the tortillas. Spoon $\frac{1}{2}$ of the chicken mixture over tortillas and sprinkle with $\frac{1}{2}$ of the cheese. Repeat layers. Cover with aluminum foil and refrigerate for at least 1 hour or overnight.

Heat oven to 350°. Bake covered for 40 minutes. Remove foil and bake until top is lightly browned, about 10 minutes.

CHINESE CHICKEN CASSEROLE

Chop suey vegetables add crunch to this flavorful casserole. Look for them in the Asian foods section of your supermarket.

1 pkg. (6.2 oz.) long grain and wild rice with seasoning packet
1 can (10.75 oz.) condensed cream of mushroom soup
1 can (14 oz.) chop suey vegetables, drained
1⅓ cups (1 soup can) hot water
4 skinless, boneless chicken breast halves, about 1 lb.
paprika

Heat oven to 350°. Combine rice, soup and vegetables in a medium bowl and mix well. Crumble contents of rice seasoning packet over mixture and stir in hot water. Spread mixture evenly in a 2-quart shallow baking dish. Place chicken breasts on top and sprinkle with paprika. Cover tightly with aluminum foil and bake for about 1 hour, until chicken is thoroughly cooked and casserole is hot and bubbly.

CHICKEN CRUNCH CASSEROLE

This easy "put together" goes great with green vegetables and tomato wedges.

1 can (3 oz.) chow mein noodles
1 can (10.75 oz.) condensed cream of celery soup
1 can (5 oz.) chunk white chicken, broken into chunks
1 jar (4.5 oz.) sliced mushrooms
$\frac{1}{2}$ cup (2 oz. pkg.) salted cashews
chopped fresh parsley or chives for garnish, optional

Heat oven to 350°. In a $1\frac{1}{2}$-quart casserole, combine $\frac{1}{2}$ of the chow mein noodles with soup, chicken chunks, mushrooms with liquid and cashews; mix well. Bake uncovered for about 25 minutes, until casserole is hot and bubbly. Sprinkle remaining noodles around the edge of casserole and bake for 5 additional minutes. Garnish with parsley or chives if desired.

VARIATION: TUNA CRUNCH CASSEROLE

Substitute 1 can (6 oz.) chunk light tuna, drained and broken into chunks, for chicken.

TUNA FLORENTINE

Servings: 4

*Serve this delicious combination over rice with a sliced tomato salad. To thaw frozen spinach quickly, refer to **Tips for Frozen Foods**, page 6.*

1 pkg. (10 oz.) frozen chopped spinach, thawed
1 can (10.75 oz.) condensed cream of mushroom soup
1 tbs. lemon juice
1 can (6 oz.) chunk light tuna, drained, broken into chunks
1 can (2.8 oz.) French fried onions

Heat oven to 350°. Place spinach in a colander and press out as much liquid as possible. In a 1½-quart shallow casserole, combine spinach with soup, lemon juice and tuna. Bake uncovered for 25 minutes. Sprinkle onions over casserole and bake for 5 additional minutes.

ORIENTAL MACARONI CASSEROLE

Servings: 6

Here's a delightfully different way to serve macaroni.

2 cans (14.75-15 oz. each) macaroni and cheese
1 can (6 oz.) chunk light tuna, drained, broken into chunks
1 can (11 oz.) Mandarin orange segments, drained
½ cup (2 oz. pkg.) salted cashews
1 can (3 oz.) chow mein noodles

Heat oven to 400°. In a lightly greased 1½-quart casserole, combine macaroni with tuna, Mandarin oranges and cashews; toss lightly together. Bake uncovered for 20 minutes or until heated through. Stir, sprinkle with chow mein noodles and bake for 5 additional minutes.

MEXICALI CASSEROLE

This quick dinner dish is perfect for a busy day. It's good served with small bowls of shredded lettuce, chopped avocado, diced onion and chopped tomato as accompaniments.

1 can (15 oz.) chili without beans
1 can (15 oz.) beef tamales with chili sauce
1 can (8.75 oz.) whole kernel golden corn, drained
1 can (2.25 oz.) sliced black olives, drained
½ cup (2 oz.) shredded sharp cheddar cheese

Heat oven to 350°. Remove any grease from the top of chili. Drain tamales, reserving sauce in a 1½-quart casserole. Stir in chili, corn and olives. Remove paper wrappings from tamales and cut each in half at an angle; discard paper. Arrange halved tamales on top of mixture. Cover casserole and bake for 20 minutes. Sprinkle with cheese and bake uncovered for 10 minutes.

CHILI-HOMINY BAKE

Hominy adds a pleasing crunch and southwestern flair to this easy casserole. Serve in soup bowls or individual casseroles.

1 can (15 oz.) chili without beans
1 can (15 oz.) chili with beans
1 can (14.5 oz.) golden or white hominy, drained
1 can (10.75 oz.) condensed cream of chicken soup
1 can (2.25 oz.) sliced black olives, drained, optional
1 cup (4 oz.) shredded sharp cheddar cheese

Heat oven to 350°. Remove any grease from the top of chili. In a 2-quart casserole, mix chili with hominy and soup. Stir in olives if desired. Cover and bake for 25 minutes. Sprinkle cheese on top of mixture and bake uncovered for 5 additional minutes, until cheese melts.

PIZZA PASTA CASSEROLE

Add zest to your pasta with pizza ingredients. For real ease, look for shredded mozzarella and cheddar that are packaged together.

2 cups (7-8 oz. pkg.) elbow macaroni
1 jar (14 oz.) pizza sauce
1 pkg. (3.5 oz.) thinly sliced pepperoni
1 jar (4.5 oz.) sliced mushrooms, drained
1 can (2.25 oz.) sliced black olives, drained
1 cup (4 oz.) shredded mozzarella cheese
1 cup (4 oz.) shredded cheddar cheese

Heat oven to 375°. Cook macaroni according to package directions; drain. In a 3-quart shallow baking dish, mix cooked macaroni, pizza sauce, pepperoni, mushrooms and black olives. Sprinkle cheese over mixture. Cover and bake for 20 minutes. Uncover and bake for 10 minutes.

GROUND BEEF AND POTATO BAKE

Easy to assemble, this layered casserole recipe makes ground beef really special fare. If you can't locate the 16-ounce package of potato nuggets, use half of a 32-ounce package (about 50 potato nuggets).

1 lb. lean ground beef
1 pkg. (0.9 oz.) dry onion-mushroom soup mix
1 can (10.75 oz.) condensed cream of celery soup
1 pkg. (16 oz.) frozen fried potato nuggets

Heat oven to 400°. Gently spread ground beef in the bottom of a 2-quart shallow baking dish. Sprinkle dry soup mix over beef and cover with cream of celery soup. Top with a single layer of potato nuggets. Bake for 35 to 40 minutes until hot and bubbly.

NO-PEEK BEEF AND GRAVY CASSEROLE

Servings: 6-8

Slow cooking results in tender beef and an enticing aroma that permeates the house. Serve this dish over noodles, rice or thick pieces of toasted bread. This can also be cooked in a crockery slow cooker on LOW for 8 to 12 hours or HIGH for 5 to 6 hours.

2 lb. cubed boneless stew beef (1-inch cubes)
1 can (10.75 oz.) condensed cream of mushroom soup
1 can (10.75 oz.) condensed French onion soup
1 can (4 oz.) mushroom stems and pieces, drained

Heat oven to 300°. Combine ingredients in a 3-quart casserole and mix well. Cover tightly with lid or aluminum foil and bake for 3 hours until beef is tender.

REUBEN DINNER CASSEROLE

A convenience potato mix keeps the preparation of this tasty dish to a minimum. To easily shred corned beef, roll slices jelly roll-style and cut crosswise into narrow strips with kitchen shears.

1 pkg. (4.5 oz.) dry julienne potatoes
1 can (8 oz.) shredded sauerkraut, well drained
2 pkg. (2.5 oz. each) thinly sliced corned beef, coarsely shredded
1 can (5 oz.) evaporated milk
2¼ cups boiling water
1 cup (4 oz.) finely shredded Swiss cheese

Heat oven to 400°. In an ungreased 8-inch square baking dish, layer potatoes, sauerkraut and corned beef. Sprinkle with cheese sauce mix from potatoes. Pour evaporated milk and water over mixture. Bake, uncovered, for 30 to 35 minutes, until potatoes are tender. Sprinkle casserole with Swiss cheese and bake for 3 to 5 minutes, until cheese melts.

ENTRÉES

VEGETABLE BURRITOS

For a nutritious, filling meal on the run, team these burritos with packaged tossed salad.

1 can (15 oz.) black beans, rinsed, drained
1 can (15.25 oz.) whole kernel golden corn, drained
1 can (14.25 oz.) Mexican-style stewed tomatoes
1 cup (4 oz.) shredded sharp cheddar cheese
8 burrito-sized flour tortillas

Heat oven to 400°. In a medium bowl, mix together beans, corn, tomatoes and $\frac{1}{2}$ cup of the shredded cheese. Spoon about $\frac{1}{2}$ cup of the mixture down the center of each tortilla. Roll tortillas up to enclose filling and place, seam-side down, in a lightly greased 9-x-13-inch baking pan. Spoon any remaining filling down the center of pan on top of rolled tortillas. Cover with aluminum foil and bake for about 10 minutes. Sprinkle remaining cheese down center of pan and return to oven for about 2 minutes, until cheese is melted.

SPAGHETTI ROMANOFF

This creamy spaghetti dish is deliciously different.

1 pkg. (8 oz.) spaghetti
1 jar (14 oz.) spaghetti sauce with mushrooms
1 pkg. (3 oz.) cream cheese, cubed
½ cup water
grated Parmesan cheese for garnish, optional

Cook spaghetti according to package directions; drain. While spaghetti is cooking, combine spaghetti sauce, cheese cubes and water in a 1-quart saucepan. Cook over medium heat, stirring constantly, until sauce is smooth and heated through. Serve sauce over drained, hot cooked spaghetti. Sprinkle with grated Parmesan cheese if desired.

FUJIYAMA TUNA

Ring hot rice on plates and fill with this Asian-style treat.

1 tbs. vegetable oil
1 can (6 oz.) chunk light tuna, drained, broken into chunks
1 pkg. (10 oz.) frozen Japanese-style vegetables with seasoned soy sauce
2 tbs. water

Heat oil in a 10-inch skillet over medium heat. Add tuna and sauté briefly. Add vegetables with sauce, and water. Bring to a full boil over high heat, separating vegetables with a fork. Reduce heat to medium, cover and cook for 4 minutes. Uncover and cook for 1 to 2 minutes, stirring occasionally.

SHRIMP GUMBO

Here's a quick version of a famous Creole dish. Serve it over hot cooked rice with sliced French bread and a tossed green salad. Pass hot pepper sauce at the table so that people can season their own dish to taste. For frozen shrimp, you can substitute 1 can (6 oz.) rinsed and drained deveined shrimp. Do not cook this dish in a iron pot or with iron utensils, as the okra will turn black.

2 cans (10.75 oz. each) condensed
   chicken gumbo soup
1 can (14.5 oz.) cut okra and tomatoes,
   or 1 can (14.5 oz.) stewed tomatoes
   with celery, green peppers and onions

½ cup water
1 pkg. (6 oz.) frozen, peeled, cleaned
   cooked shrimp
2 cups cooked white rice
hot pepper sauce, optional

In a 2-quart saucepan, combine soup with undrained okra and tomatoes and water. Heat over high heat, stirring occasionally, until mixture comes to a boil. Reduce heat to low and simmer for 5 minutes. Stir shrimp into soup mixture. Simmer, stirring often, for 1 minute or until shrimp is heated through.

To serve, mound ½ cup rice in the center of each of 4 shallow soup plates. Ladle gumbo around rice. Pass hot pepper sauce.

BAKED SOLE FILLETS

For a fantastic meal, dress up fish fillets with a delicate pink sauce and serve over rice with a green vegetable. You can substitute condensed cream of mushroom soup for the shrimp soup if desired.

1 pkg. (16 oz.) frozen sole or flounder fillets, thawed
1 can (10.75 oz.) condensed cream of shrimp soup
¼ cup (2 oz.) grated Parmesan cheese, optional
chopped fresh parsley for garnish, optional
lemon wedges for garnish, optional

Heat oven to 375°. Separate fillets and pat dry with paper towels. Arrange in a single layer in a greased 10-x-6-inch baking dish. Stir soup in can and pour evenly over fillets. Sprinkle with cheese if desired. Bake uncovered for about 25 minutes or until fish flakes easily with a fork. Garnish with chopped parsley and lemon wedges if desired. Serve immediately.

PEACHY CHICKEN AND BISCUITS

This easy-to-prepare, one-dish dinner is a dream come true for busy people.

1 pkg. (25 oz.) frozen fully-cooked fried chicken (5 to 7 pieces)
1 can (5 biscuits) refrigerated flaky buttermilk biscuits
1 can (16 oz.) cling peach halves, drained
½ cup orange marmalade

Heat oven to 375°. Arrange chicken pieces in a single layer in a 9-x-13-inch baking pan. Bake uncovered on the center oven rack for 30 minutes, turning once. Remove from oven and drain off excess fat.

Increase oven heat to 400°. Stack chicken pieces in the center of baking pan. Arrange biscuits in a single layer on one side. Place peach halves, hollow-side up, on the other side. Fill each peach half with 1 heaping tbs. orange marmalade. Bake uncovered for 10 minutes, until biscuits are golden brown.

SAVORY ROASTED CHICKEN

Use Italian salad dressing as a marinade to deliciously and effortlessly season baked chicken. You can remove the skin from the chicken if desired.

1 chicken, about 3-3½ lb., cut into serving pieces
½ cup Italian salad dressing

In a large shallow baking pan, arrange chicken pieces, skin-side up, in a single layer. Pour salad dressing over chicken pieces. Cover and marinate in the refrigerator for at least 4 hours or overnight, turning occasionally.

Heat oven to 375°. Bake chicken uncovered for 1 hour and 15 minutes, until the juices run clear when a thigh is pierced. Turn chicken several times during baking.

CRUNCHY BAKED CHICKEN

This makes a delightful entrée for guests. Serve it over hot cooked noodles, rice or mashed potatoes. You can assemble this dish up to 1 day in advance. Remove it from the refrigerator about 1 hour before baking. If using chow mein noodles, sprinkle them on just before baking. Remove the skin from the chicken if desired.

1 chicken, about 3-3½ lb., cut into serving pieces
1 can (10.75 oz.) condensed creamy chicken mushroom soup
1 cup (½ pt.) heavy whipping cream
⅓ cup (2 oz. pkg.) slivered almonds

Heat oven to 350°. In a large shallow baking pan or dish, arrange chicken pieces, skin-side up, in a single layer. In a medium bowl, blend soup with cream. Spoon soup mixture over chicken and sprinkle with almonds. Bake, uncovered, for 1 to 1½ hours, until the juices run clear when a thigh is pierced.

VARIATION: TANGY BAKED CHICKEN

Replace cream with 1 cup (8 oz. carton) sour cream mixed with 1 pkg. (1 oz.) dry onion soup mix. Replace almonds with 1 can (3 oz.) chow mein noodles.

EASY BARBECUED CHICKEN

The unexpected addition of cola tenderizes the chicken. Serve with mashed potatoes or rice to mop up the extra sauce. For an interesting twist, substitute 1 cup lemon-lime soda for the cola.

1 chicken, about 3-3½ lb., cut into serving pieces
1 bottle (14 oz.) tomato ketchup
1 cup (8 oz.) cola

To bake, heat oven to 350°. Remove skin from chicken pieces if desired. Place chicken pieces in large ovenproof skillet or 9-x-13-x-2-inch baking pan. Pour ketchup and cola over chicken and turn to coat. Bake, uncovered, for about 1 hour, until the juices run clear when a thigh is pierced.

To cook on the stovetop, bring ingredients to a boil in a 12-inch skillet or Dutch oven with a lid. Cover pan and simmer over low heat for about 45 minutes, until the juices run clear when a thigh is pierced. Remove lid and cook over medium heat 15 minutes more to thicken sauce.

To cook in a crockery slow cooker, cook on LOW for 8 to 10 hours. Remove bones before serving if desired.

SALSA CHICKEN BREASTS

This chicken, dressed up with a sauce of tomatoes, green chile peppers, onions and cilantro, is delicious served over hot cooked rice.

1 lb. skinless, boneless chicken breasts, cut into strips
1 can (15 oz.) chunky salsa-style tomato sauce

Stir-fry chicken in a 10-inch nonstick skillet over medium-high heat until lightly browned. Pour tomato sauce over chicken, cover and simmer over low heat for 10 minutes or until chicken is completely cooked.

CHICKEN STIR-FRY WITH PASTA

Servings: 4

Impress your family and friends with this rush-hour recipe.

1 lb. skinless, boneless chicken breasts, cut into strips
1 can (10.75 oz.) condensed cream of chicken soup
$\frac{2}{3}$ cup ($\frac{1}{2}$ soup can) water
1 pkg. (16 oz.) frozen seasoned pasta and vegetables

Stir-fry chicken in a 10-inch nonstick skillet over medium-high heat until lightly browned. Add soup, water and pasta-vegetable mixture. Cover and simmer over low heat for about 10 minutes, stirring often, until vegetables are tender and chicken is completely cooked.

CHICKEN POT PIE

Here's a tasty shortcut version of an old-time favorite. You can also use cubed cooked ham instead of chicken.

2 cans (10.75 oz. each) condensed cream of chicken soup
1 can (5 oz.) evaporated milk
2 cans (15 oz. each) original mixed vegetables, drained
1 pkg. (9 oz.) frozen diced cooked chicken (about 2 cups), or 1 can (10 oz.) chunk
    white chicken, broken into chunks
1 can (10 biscuits) refrigerated buttermilk biscuits

Heat oven to 400°. In a 3-quart shallow baking dish, slowly stir together soup and milk. Stir in vegetables and chicken and bake for 15 minutes. Remove dish from oven and stir. Separate biscuit dough, cut each biscuit in quarters and arrange dough portions near the outer edge of hot chicken mixture. Bake for about 15 minutes, until biscuits are golden brown.

TURKEY-VEGETABLE SKILLET DINNER

Servings: 4

Here's a different way to serve turkey for a busy night.

1 lb. ground turkey
2 pkg. (1 oz. each) dry onion soup mix
1 cup water
1 pkg. (16 oz.) frozen mixed vegetables

In a medium bowl, mix ground turkey with 1 pkg. of the onion soup mix. Shape mixture into 4 equal patties. Brown patties in a 10-inch nonstick skillet over medium-high heat; remove to a plate. Add remaining soup mix and water to skillet. Bring to a full boil over high heat and add mixed vegetables, stirring to separate. Reduce heat to low and simmer for 3 minutes, stirring once. Add patties and cook for 5 minutes, until patties are completely cooked.

SAUSAGE AND TWO-BEAN STEW

This dish is reminiscent of French "cassoulet." For a filling meal, serve it with slices of hot garlic bread. If you can't locate Great Northern beans in your supermarket, you can substitute 2 cups canned or cooked white, marrow, navy or pea beans.

1 lb. bulk pork sausage
1 can (15 oz.) red kidney beans, rinsed and drained
1 can (15 oz.) Great Northern beans, rinsed and drained
1 can (14.5 oz.) sliced carrots, drained
1 can (14.5 oz.) diced tomatoes with garlic and onions

In a 12-inch skillet or Dutch oven, cook sausage over medium heat until browned, stirring to break apart. Drain well on paper towels and return to skillet. Add remaining ingredients and cook over low heat for about 15 minutes, until heated through, stirring occasionally.

SWEET AND SPICY BAKED PORK CHOPS

Servings: 6-8

*If desired, you can use **Onion-Orange Glaze**, **Tangy Onion Glaze** or **Cranberry-Onion Glaze**, page 140, instead of the **Sweet and Spicy Sauce** for this succulent recipe.*

6-8 pork chops, ½-inch thick
Sweet and Spicy Sauce, page 139

Heat oven to 350°. In a large shallow baking pan, arrange pork chops in a single layer. Spoon sauce over pork chops. Bake, uncovered, for 1¼ hours, until pork chops are thoroughly cooked.

VARIATION: SWEET AND SPICY BAKED CHICKEN

Servings: 6-8

Substitute 1 chicken, about 3-3½ lb., cut into serving pieces, for pork chops. Bake, uncovered, skin-side up, for 1 to 1½ hours, until the juices run clear when a thigh is pierced.

PORK, RICE AND GRAVY BAKE

Servings: 6

This makes a great dinner dish for family or company.

$2\frac{1}{4}$ cups instant white rice, such as Minute Rice
1 can (10.75 oz.) condensed cream of celery soup
1 can (10.75 oz.) condensed cream of chicken soup
1 can (5 oz.) evaporated milk
1 pkg. (1.3 oz.) dry golden onion soup mix
6 bone-in pork loin chops, $\frac{1}{2}$-inch thick

Heat oven to 350°. In a greased large shallow baking pan or dish, combine rice, condensed soups, milk and $\frac{1}{2}$ of the dry soup mix. Arrange pork chops on top in a single layer and sprinkle with remaining dry soup mix. Cover pan tightly with foil and bake for 1 hour. Uncover pan and bake for 15 additional minutes, until pork chops are thoroughly cooked.

VARIATION: CHICKEN, RICE AND GRAVY BAKE

Servings: 6-8

Substitute 1 chicken, about $3-3\frac{1}{2}$ lb., cut into serving pieces, for pork chops. Bake according to pork recipe, until the juices run clear when a thigh is pierced.

BEEF NOODLE SKILLET DINNER

Servings: 4

This dish is a favorite with all ages.

1 lb. lean ground beef
1 pkg. (3 oz.) instant Oriental (ramen)
   noodle soup with beef flavor
1 can (14.5 oz.) stewed tomatoes with
   onions, celery and green peppers
1 can (8-8.75 oz.) whole kernel golden
   corn

In a 10-inch nonstick skillet, cook ground beef over medium-high heat until browned, stirring with fork to break apart. Drain well on paper towels and return to skillet. Stir in seasoning packet from oriental noodles, undrained tomatoes and corn. Bring to a boil over high heat, stirring constantly. Crumble noodles into mixture. Reduce heat to low, cover and simmer for about 10 minutes until noodles are tender. Stir after 5 minutes to separate noodles.

NO-MESS ROAST WITH RICH GRAVY

This easy cooking method produces a delicious main course roast, complete with gravy. You can serve the unthickened pan juices, skimmed of fat, for a variation of gravy if desired.

2-4 lb. boneless beef roast
1 pkg. (1 oz.) dry onion soup mix, or 1
    pkg. (1.15 oz.) dry beefy mushroom
    soup mix

flour
water

Heat oven to 375°. Place roast on a long sheet of heavy-duty aluminum foil in a shallow baking pan. Sprinkle roast on all sides with dry soup mix. Bring ends of foil up over roast and seal together with a double fold. Seal sides together with a double fold of foil to form a package; do not press foil flat against roast. Bake for 1 to 2 hours, until roast is fork-tender. Open one end of foil package and pour drippings into a small saucepan. Skim fat from the top of pan drippings.

To thicken gravy, measure reserved juices in saucepan. For each cup of liquid, combine ¼ cup water and 1 tbs. flour in a small bowl. Gradually stir flour mixture into pan drippings and cook over medium heat until mixture boils. Cook, stirring, until thickened. Reduce heat to low and cook for 5 minutes, stirring occasionally.

BUSY-DAY BRISKET

Using a crockery pot to cook beef brisket results in a tender, tasty main dish with lots of gravy. Spoon the accumulated meat juices over the cooked brisket. Provide plenty of crusty bread for mopping up the surplus.

3-5 lb. boneless beef brisket, well trimmed
1 pkg. (1 oz.) dry onion soup mix
1 jar (4.5 oz.) sliced mushrooms

If necessary, cut brisket into several pieces to fit in a crockery pot. Place meat pieces fat-side up. In a small bowl, combine onion soup mix with mushrooms and their liquid. Spread mushroom mixture evenly over the top of each brisket portion. Cover crockery pot and cook on LOW for 10 to 12 hours or until beef is tender. Remove brisket from crockery pot and cut into thin slices across the grain at a slanting angle.

SAVORY MARINATED STEAK

Use Italian salad dressing to tenderize and add flavor to your favorite cut of steak. It works well for London broil, boneless sirloin, T-bone or top loin steaks.

$^1/_2$ cup Italian salad dressing
$2^1/_2$-3 lb. steak

Pour salad dressing over steak in a shallow dish. Cover and marinate in the refrigerator for at least 4 hours or overnight, turning occasionally.

Grill or broil steak, basting frequently with salad dressing marinade until cooked to desired doneness.

CONDIMENTS, SAUCES AND TOPPINGS

ROSY PINEAPPLE RELISH

Makes about 2 cups

Add a festive appearance to poultry, ham, lamb, pork or veal with this relish. Or, use it to dress up purchased beef, chicken or turkey pies.

1 can (16 oz.) whole-berry cranberry
   sauce

1 can (8 oz.) crushed pineapple, well
   drained

Combine ingredients in a medium bowl and mix well. Cover mixture and refrigerate for several hours to blend flavors.

BAKED FRUIT RELISH

Makes about 11 cups

Bake this eye-catcher along with your entrée. It's especially good with ham.

1 can (20 oz.) pineapple chunks with
   juice
2 cans (11 oz. each) Mandarin orange
   segments

1 pkg. (12 oz.) pitted prunes
1 pkg. (6 oz.) dried apricots
1 can (21 oz.) cherry pie filling

Heat oven to 350°. In a 3-quart casserole, combine pineapple and Mandarin orange segments with prunes, apricots and cherry pie filling. Mix lightly together. Cover and bake for 1 hour. Serve warm.

EASY BARBECUE SAUCE

Makes about 2 cups

This quick sauce has real homemade flavor. Use it to baste chicken, hamburgers, spareribs or steak while broiling or grilling.

1 bottle (5 oz.) Worcestershire sauce
1 can (10.75 oz.) condensed tomato soup

In small bowl, combine ingredients and mix well.

SAVORY TOPPERS

Many of the recipes in this chapter can be served on, over or with the following:

- oven-warmed chow mein noodles
- corn chips
- *Quick Cornish Pasties*, page 39
- crackers
- toasted English muffin halves or bread slices
- baked puff pastry shells
- toasted frozen waffles
- egg dishes
- hot split biscuits or rolls
- hot sliced meat or vegetables
- hot cooked noodles
- hot cooked rice
- mashed or baked potatoes
- grilled or toasted sandwiches

"SOUPER" MUSHROOM SAUCE

Makes about 1¾ cups

Canned soup makes a good base for a variety of flavorful, quick and easy sauces.

1 can (10.75 oz.) condensed cream of chicken soup
1 jar (4.5 oz.) sliced mushrooms
1 tsp. soy sauce, optional

In a 1-quart saucepan, stir soup until smooth. Stir in mushrooms and their liquid. Heat over low heat, stirring occasionally, until heated through. If desired, stir in soy sauce.

VARIATIONS

Following the basic recipe, substitute the following condensed soups and flavorings for cream of chicken soup and soy sauce.

CURRIED MUSHROOM SAUCE

1 can (10.75 oz.) condensed cream of celery soup
1 jar (4.5 oz.) sliced mushrooms
½-1 tsp. curry powder, or to taste

SHERRIED MUSHROOM SAUCE

1 can (10.75 oz.) condensed cream of mushroom soup
1 jar (4.5 oz.) sliced mushrooms
1 tbs. dry sherry

SHRIMP AND MUSHROOM SAUCE

1 can (10.75 oz.) condensed cream of shrimp soup
1 jar (4.5 oz.) sliced mushrooms
1 tsp. prepared mustard

SPEEDY STROGANOFF SAUCE

*This sauce enhances sliced beef, hamburgers, steak sandwiches or noodles. Serve the cheese variation over **Quick Cornish Pasties**, page 39. For a quick meal, stir 1 can (6 oz.) chunk light tuna, drained, into sauce and heat through. Serve over hot cooked noodles, rice or chow mein noodles.*

1 can (10.75 oz.) condensed cream of mushroom soup
1 jar (4.5 oz.) sliced mushrooms
½ cup refrigerated French onion dip (about ½ an 8 oz. carton)

In a 1-quart saucepan, stir soup until smooth. Stir in mushrooms and their liquid. Cook over low heat, stirring occasionally, until heated through. Stir onion dip into hot mixture and heat just until mixture is heated through, but do not boil. Serve immediately.

VARIATION: CHEESY STROGANOFF SAUCE

Substitute 1 cup (4 oz.) shredded cheddar cheese for French onion dip. Stir until cheese is melted.

CHICKEN TETRAZZINI SAUCE

Makes about 3 cups

Serve this time-saver over hot cooked pasta. For a quick casserole that serves 4 to 5 people, heat broiler. Pour hot sauce over 6 ounces of hot, cooked and drained pasta in a 1½-quart casserole and mix gently but thoroughly. Sprinkle ½ cup grated Parmesan cheese over the casserole and broil for about 2 minutes, watching closely, until lightly browned. Serve immediately.

2 cans (10.5 oz. each) chicken à la king
1 jar (4.5 oz.) sliced mushrooms, drained
1 tbs. dry sherry, optional
dash nutmeg, optional

In a 2-quart saucepan, combine ingredients. Cook over medium heat, stirring often to prevent sticking, until mixture is heated through. If desired, stir in sherry and nutmeg and heat for 1 minute.

TANGY HAM AND CHEESE SAUCE

Makes about 6 cups

*This colorful combination of canned ingredients is ideal for a quick meal when served over one of the **Savory Toppers**, page 129. It's a great way to use up leftover ham.*

1 can (10.75 oz.) condensed cheddar cheese soup
$\frac{1}{2}$ cup water
1 can (20 oz.) pineapple chunks, drained
2 cups cubed ham, $\frac{1}{2}$-inch cubes
1 cup frozen petite peas, thawed

Pour soup and water into a 3-quart saucepan and stir until smooth. Gently stir in remaining ingredients. Heat through over low heat, stirring occasionally.

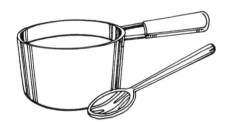

ROSY RAREBIT

Serve this over toast topped with crumbled crisp bacon, hard-cooked egg slices or sardines as a main dish for 3 to 4 people. Add the corn for a heartier dish. The **Cheesy Chicken Rarebit** *variation goes well over cooked asparagus spears on toast.*

1 can (10.75 oz.) condensed tomato soup
1 cup (4 oz.) shredded sharp cheddar cheese
¼ cup water
1 can (8-8.75 oz.) whole kernel golden corn, drained, optional

In a 1-quart saucepan, combine soup, cheese and water. Stir over low heat until cheese melts. Stir in corn, if using, until heated through.

VARIATION: CHEESY CHICKEN RAREBIT

Substitute 1 can (10.75 oz.) condensed cream of chicken soup for tomato soup. Substitute 1 can (5 oz.) chunk white chicken, drained and broken into chunks, for corn.

TOMATO RAREBIT

For an easy brunch, luncheon or supper dish for 6 to 8 people, serve this rarebit recipe over open-faced sandwiches or waffles. Some delicious suggestions for serving this sauce follow.

2 cans (10.75 oz. each) condensed cheddar cheese soup
1 can (14.5 oz.) stewed tomatoes with celery, green pepper and onions, well drained

In a 1-quart saucepan, stir soup until smooth. Stir in tomatoes. Cook over medium heat, stirring often until mixture is hot.

SERVING SUGGESTIONS

- Spoon hot mixture over toasted frozen waffles and top with crumbled crisp bacon.
- Pour hot sauce over drained canned tuna chunks on toast.
- Serve hot sauce over sliced ham and drained canned asparagus spears on toast.

QUICK PAN GRAVY

Makes about 1½ cups

If you find gravy difficult to make, this easy, pantry-shelf version will be a real favorite to serve with fried or roasted meats or poultry. You can substitute almost any condensed cream-based soup for the cream of mushroom soup, such as cream of celery, cream of chicken, beefy mushroom or chicken mushroom — whatever you have in the cupboard.

2-4 tbs. pan drippings from fried or roasted meat or poultry
1 can (10.75 oz.) condensed cream of mushroom soup
¼ cup water

Remove fried or roasted meat from skillet or roasting pan; keep warm. Remove excess fat from pan and transfer drippings to a small bowl; set aside. Pour soup into skillet or roasting pan and stir well to loosen browned bits on the bottom. Blend in water and drippings. Cook mixture over medium heat on the stovetop, stirring often until mixture is smooth and bubbly. Serve with fried or roasted meat.

CREAMY PAN GRAVY

If you are fond of fried chicken with milk gravy, try this easy version.

2-4 tbs. pan drippings from fried or roasted chicken
1 can (10.75 oz.) condensed cream of chicken soup
1 can (3 oz.) sliced mushrooms broiled in butter
1 cup (8 oz. carton) sour cream, room temperature

Remove chicken from skillet or roasting pan; keep warm. Remove excess fat from pan. Add soup to drippings in pan and stir well to loosen browned bits. Blend in undrained mushrooms. Cook over medium heat on the stovetop, stirring often, until mixture is smooth and bubbly. Stir sour cream in its carton until smooth. Add to gravy, mixing well. If desired, keep gravy warm at low heat, but do not let it boil. Serve with fried or roasted chicken.

SWEET AND SPICY SAUCE

Makes about 2½ cups

*Use this to prepare **Sweet and Spicy Baked Pork Chops** or **Chicken**, page 121, or as a basting sauce for spareribs, chicken pieces, hamburgers, chops, steaks or kabobs. It is also delicious as a hot dipping sauce for cocktail meatballs.*

1 jar (10 oz.) apricot preserves
1 cup (8 oz. bottle) Russian or sweet and spicy French salad dressing
1 pkg. (1 oz.) dry onion soup mix

In small bowl, combine all ingredients, mixing well.

To use as a glaze, brush sauce on meat or poultry throughout the last 30 minutes of grilling. If you are cooking outdoors, baste sparingly as drippings can cause flare-ups.

To serve as a hot dipping sauce, bring mixture to a boil in a small saucepan. Reduce heat to low and simmer for 10 minutes, stirring occasionally. Keep warm in a fondue pot, small casserole or chafing dish over a heating element set on low.

ONION-ORANGE GLAZE

Add pizzazz to baked chicken or pork chops with this glaze and its variations.
*See **Sweet and Spicy Baked Pork Chops** or **Chicken**, page 121.*

1 can (6 oz.) frozen orange juice concentrate, slightly thawed

1 pkg. (1 oz.) dry onion soup mix

Blend ingredients together in a small bowl.

VARIATIONS

TANGY ONION GLAZE: Substitute 1 cup (8 oz. bottle) French salad dressing for orange juice concentrate. Makes about 1 cup.

CRANBERRY-ONION GLAZE: Substitute 1 can (16 oz.) jellied cranberry sauce and 1 cup (8 oz. bottle) Catalina French salad dressing for orange juice concentrate. Makes about 2½ cups.

SEASONED BUTTER SPREAD

Makes about 1¼ cups

*Keep this mixture on hand to serve over baked potatoes or corn on the cob. Or, toss with hot cooked vegetables, rice or noodles. Try it tossed with popcorn for a new twist on a favorite snack. Or use it to prepare **Party Bread**, page 89.*

1 cup (2 sticks) softened butter or margarine
1 pkg. (1 oz.) dry onion soup mix, or 2 pkg. (0.7 oz. each) dry Italian salad
    dressing mix

In a small bowl, mix ingredients until well blended. Store covered in the refrigerator. Bring to room temperature before using.

HAM AND CHEESE SPREAD

Makes about 1¼ cups

Keep this easy-to-prepare treat on hand in the refrigerator. For breakfast or a quick snack, spread it on toasted, buttered English muffin halves and broil them 4 inches from heat for 2 to 3 minutes, until hot and bubbly. Garnish with hard cooked egg slices. Serve with tomato soup in mugs for a light meal.

1 jar (5 oz.) Old English sharp pasteurized processed cheese spread
1 can (5 oz.) chunk ham, drained, broken into chunks

In a small bowl, mix ingredients together with a fork. Cover tightly and store in the refrigerator.

PIMIENTO CHEESE SPREAD

Makes about 1⅓ cups

This recipe makes a tasty sandwich filler.

2 cups (8 oz.) shredded cheddar cheese
1 can (5 oz.) evaporated milk
1 jar (4 oz.) diced pimientos, well drained

Combine ingredients in a 1-quart saucepan, mixing well. Stir over low heat until cheese melts. Cool mixture slightly. Store tightly covered in the refrigerator until needed. Let stand at room temperature for a few minutes before spreading.

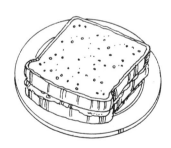

FAST FRUIT SAUCE

Makes about 1¼ cups

This sweet sauce gives a homemade taste to purchased cake, pastries, waffles, ice cream, puddings and fruit. It is also appealing layered with ice cream in parfait glasses.

1 jar (12 oz.) apricot, berry or cherry jam or preserves
lemon juice to taste, optional

In a 1-quart saucepan, heat jam or preserves over low heat, stirring occasionally, until melted. Stir in lemon juice if desired. Serve warm.

CREAMY FRESH FRUIT SAUCE

Makes about 2 cups

Serve this sauce as a topping for fresh fruit, gelatin salads or shortcake. It's also good used as a dip for fresh fruit and cookies.

1 pkg. (8 oz.) cream cheese, softened
1 jar (7 oz.) marshmallow creme

In a medium bowl, combine ingredients. Mix with an electric mixer on medium speed until well blended.

LEMON CREAM SAUCE

Makes about 2¼ cups

*Use this tangy topping to highlight chilled fruit cocktail or mixed fruit salad. It lends itself to many tasty salad and dessert variations. Try the **Orange Mayonnaise Sauce** variation on cole slaw or Waldorf salad.*

2 cups (16 oz. carton) sour cream
1 can (6 oz.) frozen lemonade concentrate, slightly thawed
dash salt, optional

Combine ingredients in a small bowl; mix well.

VARIATIONS

LEMON COCONUT SAUCE: Substitute 1 can (15 oz.) cream of coconut for sour cream. Shake well before opening can. Makes about 2 cups.

ORANGE MAYONNAISE SAUCE: Substitute 2 cups mayonnaise for sour cream; substitute 1 can (6 oz.) frozen orange juice concentrate, slightly thawed, for lemonade concentrate. Makes about 2⅔ cups.

RASPBERRY SAUCE

Makes about 1 cup

*Serve over lemon sherbet, ice cream or **Minute Melba**, page 150. The rich red color complements all berries as well as cantaloupe and honeydew melon.*

1 pkg. (10 oz.) frozen raspberries, partially thawed
lemon juice to taste, optional

Spoon raspberries with syrup and lemon juice, if using, into a blender container. Cover and blend at low speed for 45 seconds or until smooth. Strain if desired to remove seeds.

MINCEMEAT BREAKFAST SAUCE

Makes about 2⅓ cups

Dress up frozen French toast, pancakes or waffles with this tasty, convenient sauce.

1 jar (11.5-12 oz.) orange marmalade
1⅓ cups (about ½ a 27 oz. jar) mincemeat

Combine ingredients in a 2-quart saucepan. Cook over low heat, stirring constantly, for 5 minutes or until mixture is well blended and bubbly. Serve warm.

CHOCOLATE SAUCE

This quick sauce is delicious served over ice cream, pudding, cake, cream puffs or canned pear halves.

1 cup (6 oz. pkg.) semisweet chocolate chips
1 can (5 oz.) evaporated milk

In a 2-quart heavy saucepan or the top part of a double boiler, combine chocolate chips and milk. Cook over low heat or simmering water, stirring, just until chocolate is melted and mixture is smooth. Serve warm.

Makes about 2 cups

VARIATION: FLUFFY CHOCOLATE SAUCE

Add 1 jar (7 oz.) marshmallow creme to chocolate chips and milk. Serve warm or cold.

DESSERTS

SPICED FRUIT COMPOTE

Serve this compote over squares of cake and scoops of vanilla ice cream. Serve warmed leftovers as a relish with ham or pork. Reserve fruit syrups for later use in beverages, gelatin salads, dessert sauces or meat glazes.

1 can (17 oz.) apricot halves, well drained
1 can (29 oz.) cling peach halves, well drained
1 can (29 oz.) pear halves, well drained
1 can (20 oz.) pineapple chunks, well drained
1 can (16 oz.) applesauce
6 tbs. butter or margarine
ground ginger to taste

Heat oven to 350°. Arrange apricots, peaches, pears and pineapple chunks in a 3-quart shallow baking dish and cover with applesauce. Dot with butter or margarine and sprinkle lightly with ground ginger. Bake for about 45 minutes. Serve warm.

MINUTE MELBA

*This quick version of peach Melba can easily be doubled or tripled to serve a crowd. It looks pretty served in goblets or sherbet glasses. Substitute **Raspberry Sauce**, page 146, for the raspberries if desired.*

1 can (16 oz.) cling peach halves, chilled, drained
2 cups (1 pt.) vanilla ice cream
1 pkg. (10 oz.) frozen raspberries, thawed
slivered or sliced almonds for garnish, optional

Place 1 peach half in each serving dish with the hollow side up. Top each peach half with a scoop of ice cream and a spoonful of raspberries. Garnish with almonds if desired. Serve immediately.

FRUIT CRUMB COBBLER

Cake mix makes a surprisingly delicious crusty golden brown topping.

1 can (20 oz.) crushed pineapple with juice, or 1 can (15.25 oz.) pineapple chunks
   with juice
1 can (21 oz.) cherry or blueberry pie filling
1 pkg. (18 oz.) yellow, lemon or white cake mix
1 cup (2 sticks) cold butter or stick margarine, thinly sliced
vanilla ice cream or whipped cream, optional

Heat oven to 375°. Pour undrained pineapple into a 9-x-13-inch baking pan and top with pie filling. Sprinkle cake mix evenly over filling. Dot with butter, but do not stir. Bake for 35 to 40 minutes, until top is golden brown. Serve warm, topped with a scoop of ice cream or whipped cream if desired.

APPLE CINNAMON COBBLER

This is a shortcut version of an old favorite. Substitute peach, pineapple or any other flavor pie filling for the apple pie filling.

1 can (21 oz.) apple pie filling
1 can (12.4 oz.) refrigerated cinnamon rolls with icing

Heat oven to 375°. Pour pie filling into a 9-inch pie pan. Separate cinnamon roll dough and cut each dough portion into 2 semicircles. Place 9 of the dough halves, topping-side up, on top of filling around the edge of pan with the sides touching. Arrange 5 dough halves in a circle inside outer row; place 2 dough halves in the center. Bake, uncovered, for 20 to 25 minutes, until rolls are golden brown. Remove from oven and spread icing over top. Spoon warm cobbler onto individual dessert dishes.

APPLE CRISP

Use your imagination to create other delicious flavor combinations, such as apple pie filling with spice cake mix and pecans or walnuts; peach pie filling with yellow cake mix and almonds; or pineapple pie filling with white cake mix and coconut. Serve warm or cold topped with ice cream, whipping cream, or whipped dessert topping, if desired.

1 can (21 oz.) apple pie filling
1 pkg. (9 oz.) yellow cake mix, or 1/2 an 18 oz. pkg.
1/2 cup (2 oz. pkg.) nut pieces, optional
1/2 cup (1 stick) cold butter or stick margarine, thinly sliced

Heat oven to 350°. Pour pie filling into an 8- or 9-inch square baking pan. Sprinkle cake mix evenly over filling and top with nuts, if using. Dot butter or margarine evenly over top; do not stir. Bake for 40 to 45 minutes, until top is golden brown. Spoon into individual dessert dishes.

FROZEN STRAWBERRY SHORTCAKE

Keep this dessert on hand in your freezer for unexpected guests. Try other ice cream and topping combinations such as butter pecan ice cream with chocolate sauce. Instead of strawberries, you can substitute strawberry ice cream topping or blueberry or cherry pie filling.

1 pkg. (16 oz.) frozen baked loaf pound cake
1 pt. vanilla ice cream, slightly softened
1 pkg. (10 oz.) frozen sliced strawberries, partially thawed

With a long, serrated knife, slice frozen cake horizontally into 2 equal layers. Spread ice cream evenly over 1 cake layer and cover with remaining layer. Gently press layers together. Wrap filled cake with aluminum foil so that it is airtight. Freeze for at least 8 hours before serving.

To serve, let cake stand at room temperature for 10 minutes. Cut cake into 12 slices and spoon strawberries and syrup over each serving. Serve immediately.

CHOCOLATE TORTE

Store this sophisticated dessert in the freezer, ready for company. When slicing cake into layers, measure even widths with a ruler and insert wooden picks as markers around the cake. Using picks as a guide, slice through the cake with a long-bladed serrated knife with a light sawing motion. To melt chocolate chips in the microwave, place them in a glass bowl and heat on HIGH for 1 minute. Stir and heat in 10-second intervals, stirring with a fork until smooth.

1 pkg. (16 oz.) frozen baked loaf pound cake
1 pkg. (12 oz.) semisweet chocolate chips
1 cup (8 oz. carton) sour cream, room temperature

With a long, serrated knife, slice frozen cake horizontally into 6 equal layers. In a 2-quart heavy saucepan over low heat or the top of a double boiler over simmering water, heat chocolate chips, stirring until chocolate begins to melt. Remove from heat and stir. Heat for a few seconds at a time, stirring until smooth. When chocolate is smooth, remove from heat and cool for 10 minutes. Fold in sour cream until well blended. Separate cake layers and spread chocolate mixture evenly between each layer. With a spatula, reassemble layers using the cardboard lid of pound cake package as a base. Gently press filled cake together. Wrap cake in aluminum foil so that it is airtight. Freeze for at least 4 hours. Cut into slices to serve.

JIFFY CHOCOLATE FONDUE

Canned frosting can be used to make a quick chocolate dessert fondue or party dip. Place a tray of assorted cake and fruit dippers in the freezer for 30 to 60 minutes until icy cold. This makes it easier for the fondue to coat them. Serve with a tray of 3 or 4 types of dippers. Let guests spear dippers with fondue forks or bamboo skewers, and swirl them into the chocolate fondue. Allow 8 to 12 dippers per person. Leftover fondue is good served hot or cold over ice cream or squares of cake.

1 can (16 oz.) ready-to-spread chocolate frosting
1 tbs. brandy or Kirsch, optional

In an electric fondue pot or 1-quart heavy saucepan, heat frosting over low heat, stirring frequently until heated through. If desired, stir in brandy or Kirsch just before serving. Keep warm over low heat in fondue pot, or in a candle-warmed ceramic fondue pot. Take care not to raise heat too high, or it will scorch the chocolate and burn mouths.

SUGGESTED DIPPERS

- angel food, chiffon, pound or sponge cake, cut into cubes
- purchased doughnuts or lady-fingers, cut into 1-inch pieces
- maraschino cherries, well drained
- canned Bing cherries, well drained
- canned Mandarin orange segments, well drained
- canned pineapple chunks, well drained
- whole pitted dates, dried apricots or prunes
- crystallized ginger pieces
- marshmallows
- large salted nuts
- popcorn
- pretzel twists
- fresh fruit pieces

CREAM OF COCONUT CAKE

Servings: 12-16

This recipe makes a very moist cake. You can also use 1 pkg. (18.5 oz.) lemon, white or yellow cake mix. Prepare cake as directed on package and bake in a 9-x-13-inch baking pan. When done, poke holes down through cake with a 2-prong utility fork at ½-inch intervals to allow milk mixture to soak into the cake. Proceed with recipe.

1 pkg. (16 oz.) frozen baked pound cake
1 can (14 oz.) sweetened condensed milk
1 can (8.5 oz.) cream of coconut
1 pkg. (7 oz.) flaked coconut
1 pkg. (8 oz.) frozen whipped dessert topping, thawed

With a serrated knife, slice pound cake vertically into 12 slices and line the bottom of a 9-x-13-inch baking dish with 2 rows of 6 slices each. In a small bowl, combine sweetened condensed milk and cream of coconut. Pour over cake, allowing mixture to soak for about 30 minutes. In a small bowl, fold 1 cup of the flaked coconut into whipped topping and spread over cake. Sprinkle with remaining coconut. Cover and chill in the refrigerator overnight. Cut into squares to serve.

EASY APPLE PIE

This variation of a family favorite has a homemade appearance. For a sweet crust, sprinkle top with granulated sugar before baking.

1 pkg. frozen deep dish pie crusts (two
    9-inch crusts)
2 jars (23 oz. each) chunky applesauce, or
    1 can (30 oz.) apple pie filling
1 tsp. cinnamon, optional
frozen whipped dessert topping, thawed,
    optional

Heat oven to 425°. Prepare pie crusts according to package directions for a double crust pie, using applesauce as a filling. Sprinkle with cinnamon if desired. Cut several slits in top crust to allow steam to escape. Place on a baking sheet and bake for 10 minutes. Reduce oven heat to 350° and bake for 25 to 35 minutes, until crust is golden brown. Cool completely before cutting. Serve warmed or cooled, topped with whipped topping if desired.

ICE CREAM SUNDAE PIE

Dress up ice cream pie with classic sundae toppings. To cut the pie easily, run hot water over a long knife and wipe dry with a towel before cutting. Repeat as needed. To quickly soften ice cream, heat in the microwave on HIGH for 10 to 30 seconds.

4 cups (1 qt.) vanilla ice cream, softened
1 prepared chocolate crumb pie crust, 9-inch size
1 jar (12 oz.) hot fudge topping, unheated
½ cup (2 oz. pkg.) nut pieces
frozen whipped dessert topping, thawed, optional
maraschino cherries for garnish, optional

Spoon ice cream into crust. Cover and freeze for 2 to 3 hours, until firm. To serve, cut pie into wedges with a hot knife. Spoon fudge topping generously over each serving; sprinkle with nuts. Garnish with a spoonful of whipped topping and a cherry, if desired.

LEMONADE PIE

This recipe is creamy, delicious and "easy as pie" to make. You can use frozen limeade concentrate for an appealing variation. For a more colorful appearance, a few drops of food color can be added to the mixture. Use yellow with lemonade or green with limeade.

1 can (14 oz.) sweetened condensed milk
1 can (6 oz.) frozen lemonade concentrate, partially thawed
1 pkg. (8 oz.) frozen whipped dessert topping, thawed
1 prepared graham cracker pie crust, 9-inch size

In a medium bowl, combine sweetened condensed milk, lemonade concentrate and whipped topping. Mix well with a fork or wire whisk. Spoon mixture into crust. Cover and freeze until filling is set, at least 8 hours. Remove pie from freezer about 5 minutes before serving. Cut into wedges to serve.

LEMON CHEESECAKE PIE

This makes a lovely ending for a special dinner. You can use canned blueberry or cherry pie filling, or any fresh or frozen fruit in place of the strawberries.

1 can (12 oz.) lemon ready-to-spread whipped frosting
1 carton (8 oz.) small curd cottage cheese
1 cup (8 oz. carton) sour cream
1 prepared graham cracker pie crust, 10-inch size
1 pkg. (10 oz.) frozen sliced strawberries, just thawed

In a large bowl, combine frosting, cottage cheese and sour cream and stir until well blended. Spread filling in crust. Cover and freeze overnight.

To serve, let pie stand in the refrigerator for about 30 minutes, until it is easy to cut, but still slightly firm. Cut into wedges and spoon strawberries over each serving.

TROPICAL CREAM PIE

Garnish this pie with additional whipped topping and fruit if desired. For a change of pace, substitute 2 cartons (8 oz. each) strawberry yogurt for the sherbet. For a more colorful appearance, a few drops of food coloring can be added to the filling.

2 cups (1 pt.) pineapple or orange sherbet, softened
1 pkg. (8 oz.) frozen whipped dessert topping, thawed
1 prepared graham cracker pie crust, 9-inch size

In a large bowl, stir sherbet gently into whipped topping until well blended. Spoon mixture into crust. Cover and freeze for at least 4 hours or overnight, until firm. Let stand at room temperature for 15 minutes or until pie can be easily cut.

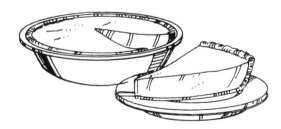

CHOCOLATE ALMOND PIE

Using candy bars offers a convenient shortcut to the preparation of chocolate pie.

2 bars (4 oz.) milk chocolate candy with almonds, broken into pieces
1 pkg. (8 oz.) frozen whipped dessert topping, thawed
1 prepared graham cracker pie crust, 9-inch size

In a 2-quart heavy saucepan or the top part of a double boiler, melt chocolate bars over low heat or simmering water. Cool. Stir whipped topping into cooled chocolate mixture until well mixed. Spoon mixture into crust. Cover and refrigerate for at least 2 hours, until well chilled. Cut into wedges to serve.

FUDGING FUDGE

This shortcut for fudge is perfect for busy people with a sweet tooth. To make it in a microwave, place chocolate chips, peanut butter and sweetened condensed milk in a 3-quart microwaveable bowl. Cook on HIGH for 2½ to 3 minutes, until melted, stirring after each minute. Proceed with recipe.

1 pkg. (12 oz.) semisweet chocolate or butterscotch chips
1 jar (12 oz.) creamy or chunky peanut butter
1 can (14 oz.) sweetened condensed milk
½ cup (2 oz. pkg.) chopped nuts, optional

Line an 8-inch square pan with waxed paper, letting waxed paper hang slightly over 2 sides. In a 3-quart heavy saucepan, combine chocolate chips, peanut butter and sweetened condensed milk. Stir over low heat until chocolate is melted. Remove from heat. Quickly stir in nuts, if using. Spread mixture evenly into prepared pan and refrigerate for about 2 hours, until firm.

Grasp waxed paper and remove fudge from pan in one block. Turn out onto a cutting board and peel off waxed paper. Cut fudge into 1-inch squares. Store in a covered container at room temperature.

ROCKY ROAD FUDGE

This candy is so easy to make, why not make several batches to give as gifts? To make this in a microwave, place chocolate chips and sweetened condensed milk in a 3-quart microwavable bowl. Microwave on HIGH for 2 minutes or until chocolate is melted, stirring with a fork after 1 minute. Proceed with recipe.

1 pkg. (12 oz.) semisweet chocolate chips
1 can (14 oz.) sweetened condensed milk
1 pkg. (10.5 oz.) miniature white marshmallows
1/2 cup (2 oz. pkg.) walnut pieces

Line an 8-inch square pan with waxed paper, letting waxed paper hang slightly over 2 sides. In a 3-quart heavy saucepan, combine chocolate chips and sweetened condensed milk. Stir over low heat until chocolate melts and mixture is smooth. Remove from heat. Quickly add marshmallows and walnuts, stirring gently until evenly coated with chocolate. Spread mixture evenly in prepared pan and refrigerate for about 2 hours, until firm.

Grasp waxed paper and remove fudge from pan in one block. Turn out onto a cutting board and peel off waxed paper. Cut fudge into 1-inch squares. Store in a covered container at room temperature.

INDEX

SERVE CREATIVE, EASY, NUTRITIOUS MEALS WITH nitty gritty® COOKBOOKS

Beer and Good Food
Unbeatable Chicken Recipes
Gourmet Gifts
From Freezer, 'Fridge and Pantry
Edible Pockets for Every Meal
Cooking With Chile Peppers
Oven and Rotisserie Roasting
Risottos, Paellas and Other Rice
  Specialties
Entrées From Your Bread Machine
Muffins, Nut Breads and More
Healthy Snacks for Kids
100 Dynamite Desserts
Recipes for Yogurt Cheese
Sautés
Cooking in Porcelain
Appetizers
Casseroles
The Toaster Oven Cookbook
Skewer Cooking on the Grill
Creative Mexican Cooking
Extra-Special Crockery Pot Recipes
Slow Cooking
Marinades
The Wok

No Salt, No Sugar, No Fat Cookbook
Quick and Easy Pasta Recipes
Cooking in Clay
Deep Fried Indulgences
Cooking with Parchment Paper
The Garlic Cookbook
From Your Ice Cream Maker
Cappuccino/Espresso: The Book of
  Beverages
The Best Pizza is made at home*
The Best Bagels are made at home*
Convection Oven Cookery
The Steamer Cookbook
The Pasta Machine Cookbook
The Versatile Rice Cooker
The Dehydrator Cookbook
The Bread Machine Cookbook
The Bread Machine Cookbook II
The Bread Machine Cookbook III
The Bread Machine Cookbook IV:
  Whole Grains and Natural Sugars
The Bread Machine Cookbook V:
  Favorite Recipes from 100 Kitchens

The Bread Machine Cookbook VI:
  *Hand-Shaped Breads from the
  Dough Cycle*
Worldwide Sourdoughs From Your
  Bread Machine
Recipes for the Pressure Cooker
The New Blender Book
The Sandwich Maker Cookbook
Waffles
Indoor Grilling
The Coffee Book
The Juicer Books I and II
Bread Baking (traditional)
The 9x13 Pan Cookbook
Recipes for the Loaf Pan
Low Fat American Favorites
Healthy Cooking on the Run
Favorite Seafood Recipes
New International Fondue Cookbook
Favorite Cookie Recipes
Flatbreads From Around the World
Cooking for 1 or 2
The Well Dressed Potato

For a free catalog, write or call:
Bristol Publishing Enterprises, Inc.
P.O. Box 1737, San Leandro, CA 94577
(800) 346-4889; in California, (510) 895-4461

* perfect for your bread
machine